A CENTURY OF SCULPTURE
THE **NASHER**
COLLECTION

Curated by

CARMEN GIMÉNEZ

STEVEN A. NASH

GUGGENHEIM MUSEUM
FINE ARTS MUSEUMS OF SAN FRANCISCO

MASTERWORKS OF MODERN SCULPTURE:
THE NASHER COLLECTION

Fine Arts Museums of San Francisco
California Palace of the Legion of Honor
October 1996–January 1997

A CENTURY OF SCULPTURE:
THE NASHER COLLECTION

Solomon R. Guggenheim Museum, New York
February–April 1997

This exhibition is co-organized by the Solomon R. Guggenheim Museum
and the Fine Arts Museums of San Francisco.

Generous support for the exhibition in San Francisco has been provided by Mr. and Mrs. Robert McNeil,
Bobbie and Mike Wilsey, Mr. and Mrs. Peter Joost, and McCutchen, Doyle, Brown & Enersen, LLP.

Some of the works in the exhibition are owned by The Nasher Foundation.

CATALOGUE
Designed by Juan Ariño
Assisted by Marta Elorriaga

© 1996 The Solomon R. Guggenheim Foundation, New York. All rights reserved.
Michael Brenson's essay © 1996 Michael Brenson.
ISBN 0-8109-6898-3 (hardcover)
ISBN 0-89207-178-8 (softcover)
Printed in Italy by Arnoldo Mondadori Editore S.p.A.

Guggenheim Museum Publications
1071 Fifth Avenue
New York, New York 10128

Hardcover edition distributed by
Harry N. Abrams, Inc.
100 Fifth Avenue
New York, New York 10011

PHOTO CREDITS
All photographs by David Heald except the following:
pp. 18, 22, 30, 31: courtesy of Raymond Nasher; p. 79: Joseph McDonald; pp. 109, 155, 205, 259: Robert Newcombe,
© The Nelson Gallery Foundation; pp. 175, 262–63: Tom Jenkins; p. 181: Larry Bercow; p. 189: Rafael Lobato;
pp. 207, 209, 223, 277, 290–91, 295, 303, 309: Lee Clockman; p. 271: Nic Tenwiggenhorn, courtesy of Oil & Steel Gallery;
p. 293: Prudence Cuming Associates Ltd., courtesy of Waddington Galleries; p. 313: Douglas M. Parker Studio,
courtesy of the artist; pp. 314–15: Walker Art Center, Minneapolis.

PREFACE. **THOMAS KRENS AND HARRY S. PARKER III**

It is not hyperbole to state that the Patsy R. and Raymond D. Nasher Collection represents the finest assemblage of Modern sculpture in private hands anywhere in the world. Since its beginnings in the mid-1960s with the purchase of works by Jean Arp, Barbara Hepworth, and Henry Moore, the collection has grown steadily not only in size but also in quality and depth of historical representation. It now is without peer. For Raymond Nasher and his wife, Patsy, the collection was a shared passion involving countless hours of research, travel, discussion with artists and others in the art world, and the creative pleasure of the installation of works in and around their home in Dallas. Paramount to their collecting interests was the joy of living with the sculptures on a daily basis. As Patsy Nasher once expressed it, "The works acquired us; we didn't acquire them."

Following Mrs. Nasher's death in 1988, Raymond Nasher continued to build the collection with acquisitions that both extended its reach into contemporary art and rounded out its historical coverage. It now numbers more than three hundred works. From Paul Gauguin and Auguste Rodin to such contemporary artists as Magdalena Abakanowicz and Richard Serra, the Nasher Collection highlights many of the artists and different stylistic languages that have marked so strongly the visual and intellectual adventure of avant-garde sculpture over the past century. The collection was not put together, however, as an exercise in art history. It reveals very clearly the personal tastes and enthusiasms of the individuals who shaped it. Most notable in this regard is the representation of certain key artists in great depth: Alberto Giacometti, Raymond Duchamp-Villon, Henri Matisse, Pablo Picasso, and David Smith, among others, are represented with multiple works, tracing different thematic concerns and periods of development. Also unique to the philosophy behind the collection is the ongoing commitment to share the collection with as broad a public as possible through exhibitions and loans and also installations in different public spaces, from museums to commercial and government settings. As Raymond Nasher explains in the interview published in this volume, this dedication to sharing goes hand in hand with the notion that art can make a major difference in people's daily lives.

It is an honor and a pleasure to be able to present selections from this fine collection to museum audiences in New York and San Francisco. From the outset, the exhibition has been a joint project between the Solomon R. Guggenheim Museum and the Fine Arts Museums of San Francisco. Our respective curators-in-charge are Carmen Giménez, Curator of Twentieth-Century Art, and Steven Nash, Associate Director and Chief Curator. They have been assisted in the planning and presentation of the exhibition by extremely able teams at both museums, individually thanked in the accompanying acknowledgments. We are also pleased to acknowledge Michael Brenson, independent critic and curator, for his perceptive essay. Financial support for the project in San Francisco came from the following sponsors: Mr. and Mrs. Robert McNeil, Bobbie and Mike Wilsey, Mr. and Mrs. Peter Joost, and McCutchen, Doyle, Brown & Enersen, LLP.

Most important, we wish to thank Raymond Nasher for his generosity in allowing us to present these masterworks of Modern sculpture, and for his support of the exhibition in so many different ways. We know that the public will share our enthusiastic appreciation of the Nasher Collection.

ACKNOWLEDGMENTS. CARMEN GIMÉNEZ AND STEVEN A. NASH

Sculpture exhibitions, due to the nature of the medium, are generally more complicated to organize than shows of two-dimensional objects. Photographing sculpture is more difficult, issues of crating, transportation, and mounting are considerably more complex, conservation always involves challenges, and the spatial dynamics of installations that must be plotted months in advance of the actual exhibition test a curator's creativity and powers of foresight. All of these concerns translate into higher than average costs, with the result that funding becomes an ever-present issue. Moreover, sculpture tends to be an art form less well known to general audiences than painting and perhaps more difficult to fully comprehend, making presentation and educational approaches all the more critical.

Despite such inherent difficulties, the organization of this exhibition has been a true pleasure, thanks to the phenomenal depth and quality of the Patsy R. and Raymond D. Nasher Collection and the encouragement and constant support provided by Raymond Nasher. Due to the extensiveness of the collection's holdings of Modern sculpture, which now number well in excess of three hundred works, problems of determining what would not be on the loan list exceeded those of what would be there. The need for reasons of space to limit ourselves in terms of numbers of works and to eliminate from consideration some of the largest and most powerful sculptures in the collection made for painful choices. Discussions between Mr. Nasher and ourselves and the analyses of individual works, which benefited also from the insights of guest essayist Michael Brenson, were an ongoing source of intellectual stimulation. For all that he meant to the project, we owe Raymond Nasher an especially profound debt of thanks.

The directors of our respective museums, Thomas Krens at the Solomon R. Guggenheim Museum and Harry S. Parker III at the Fine Arts Museums of San Francisco, also played key roles on the organizational team. Both know the Nasher Collection well, recognized the exciting potentials for a museum exhibition, and worked diligently through the logistical planning. We greatly appreciate their support and facilitating vision.

Given the many complications involved in the project, it could not have been realized so successfully without the dedicated involvement of a great many other individuals. In Dallas, several of Mr. Nasher's staff members devoted endless hours to organizational details. Ellen Gordesky and Karen Roden provided cataloguing information, photographs, crate lists, and insurance values, helped organize new photography, oversaw the crate-making and packing process, and served as general exhibition enablers. Annette Williams, Mr. Nasher's secretary, facilitated communications between the organizing parties. Elliot Cattarulla, Executive Director of the Nasher Foundation, also provided invaluable help with many logistical matters. John Dennis, conservator for the collection, carried out numerous conservation treatments in order to prepare works for exhibition, with highly successful results. Margaret and David Hendrix helped tirelessly with the art handling.

At the Guggenheim Museum, many individuals have provided invaluable assistance, starting with David Heald, Chief Photographer, Manager of Photographic Services, who did a splendid job photographing most of the works reproduced in the catalogue; he was helped by Sally Ritts, Photography and Permissions Associate. We extend our special gratitude to Lynne Addison, Exhibitions Registrar, who organized all the complex transportation arrangements. Peter Costa, former Project Services Manager/Exhibition Design Coordinator; Jocelyn Groom, Assistant Exhibition Design Coordinator; Joseph Adams, Senior Exhibition Technician; Scott Wixon, Manager of Art Services and Preparations; Peter Read, Production Services Manager/Exhibition Design Coordinator; Adrienne Shulman, Lighting Designer; and their teams provided invaluable help with the installation and lighting of the exhibition. Special thanks go to Paul Schwartzbaum, Chief Conservator, Guggenheim Museums, for his ongoing advice and expertise, as well as Eleanora Nagy, Assistant Conservator for Sculpture. Tracey Bashkoff, Curatorial Assistant, handled many curatorial aspects of the exhibition. For their essential contributions, we thank Judith Cox, General Counsel; Rosemarie Garipoli, Deputy Director for External Affairs; Lisa Dennison, Curator of Collections and Exhibitions; George McNeely, Director of Corporate and Foundation Giving; Melanie Forman, Director of Individual Giving; Stacy Bolton, Development Assistant; and Nicole Hepburn, Exhibition Administration Coordinator. Our appreciation goes to Marilyn JS Goodman, Director of Education. The catalogue was produced by the Guggenheim's Publications Department, largely through the skillful efforts of Elizabeth Levy, Managing Editor. We also thank Edward Weisberger, Editor, who prepared the text for publication, as well as Anthony Calnek, Director of Publications; Susan Lee, Media Systems Assistant/Design Assistant; and Carol Fitzgerald, Assistant Editor.

Of individuals outside the Guggenheim Museum, we thank Danielle Tilkin for her assistance in the coordination of both the exhibition and the catalogue. We especially thank Juan Ariño for his installation and catalogue design, in which endeavors he was assisted by Marta Elorriaga.

At the Fine Arts Museums of San Francisco, the following staff members provided invaluable support. Elisabeth Cornu, Head Objects Conservator, advised on conservation treatments, maintained scrupulous condition records, supervised the mounting of individual works, and oversaw the physical handling of works during installation and deinstallation; Bill White, Director of Exhibition and Technical Production, collaborated on the installation layout and design and supervised all aspects of the installation process; Bill Huggins, Engineer, installed the exhibition lighting; Therese Chen, Director of Registration, handled the myriad details of transportation and insurance; Ron Rick, Chief Graphic Designer, designed all exhibition signage and graphics; Vas Prabhu, Director of Education, and Jean Chaitin, Adult Programs Director, organized various interpretive programs, including a day-long symposium on Modern sculpture; Kathe Hodgson, Exhibitions Coordinator, coordinated the planning for the show; Paula March, Deputy Director for Marketing and Membership, and Barbara Boucke, Deputy Director for Development, assisted with fund raising and the organization of opening events; Suzy Peterson, Secretary to the Chief Curator, prepared loan lists and manuscript for the catalogue. To the following individuals and groups who provided funding for the presentation of the exhibition in San Francisco, we are especially grateful: Mr. and Mrs. Robert McNeil, Bobbie and Mike Wilsey, Mr. and Mrs. Peter Joost, and McCutchen, Doyle, Brown & Enersen, LLP. American Industrial Partners also provided support.

CONTENTS

INTRODUCTION. CARMEN GIMÉNEZ

Exhibiting sculpture from the Patsy R. and Raymond D. Nasher Collection—a selection of works that encompasses practically the entire twentieth century—makes it possible to examine the artists and works most representative of Modernist art. It is not easy to deal with art so historically close to us, and even more difficult if we focus on sculpture, the artistic genre that has suffered the deepest identity crisis over the course of our modern era. A model of classical art, sculpture has been under constant attack, the subject of polemics, practically since Romanticism. Traditionally associated with the statue, and once the classic monument par excellence, sculpture now lacks all its respected historical attributes, whether symbolic, aesthetic, technical, or material. Today we can call anything sculpture because the expansion of what is signified by the word "sculpture" authorizes it.

I wondered if, having reached this challenging point of uncertainty, we had not arrived at the appropriate moment to take stock, to review historically what had happened to sculpture, and to reflect critically on what it may mean. As I considered these matters, I recalled Sacha Guitry's film *Si Versailles m'était conté* (*Royal Affairs in Versailles*), in which the French *auteur* tried to recover the hidden secrets that live in the walls and gardens of Louis XIV's palace. The dramatic core of Guitry's film is the narration of things that were never officially told—to do so might not have been politically correct or exemplary in human terms, or it might have diminished the charisma essential to royalty. To achieve his narrative goal, Guitry used any and every evocative place, object, or circumstance as supports, among them—why not?—the innumerable statues that lined the luxurious gardens designed by André Le Nôtre.

I would like to take Guitry's idea seriously and suggest the possibility of reviewing this magnificent group of sculptural works, representative of the Nasher Collection, inquiring into their secrets, imagining what they conceal within themselves. I would like to deal with these works obliquely, from the margin of everything officially said and written about them. In a way, this was my intention when I selected the pieces now being exhibited, and it naturally oriented their installation. This approach would not have come to mind unless the Nasher Collection not only existed but also was, above all, what it is.

What would these twentieth-century sculptures speak to us about if they could do so? Not, of course, about "isms"; the myriad avant-garde movements do not fit inside them or do so only with too many difficulties. This explains the resentment of formalist twentieth-century art historiographers toward avant-garde sculpture. And, for their part, I doubt the works would want to talk to us in the definitive, rationalized terms used by a certain kind of formalism to explain their existence—even when that existence was originally stated in terms of a rigorous history of positive reductions, in which the sum of the negatives produced an affirmative. Nor do I believe that their confessions would revolve around their ghostly condition—a finality without end, a state in which all encounters, even beyond forms, would be possible, and in which sculpture would be the last remaining channel of intuition.

Again, what could these works speak to us about? Indeed, how do we imagine they would be able to speak to us? We must concentrate on the tone, modulation, and direction of the discourse. In dealing with the clamorous crisis of the statue—a crisis Rosalind E. Krauss has succinctly described as the "loss of the pedestal"—we cannot forget that it entails a renunciation of a speaker's podium, and, for that very reason, a loss of a capacity for public discourse. The orator no longer speaks *ex cathedra* but must do so within the crowd, which necessarily transforms what is said into a discussion, a dramatic conversation, or, at times, into a melodrama. What is discussed in the street must be spoken among cries and whispers, above all, causing a hubbub; it is a multitudinous conversation smashed into a thousand pieces.

Long before Gothic novels were invented, there were many classical examples of enchanted statues speaking without moving their lips. Their message was threatening and allowed no rebuttal. I am thinking, for example, about the statue of the Commendatore in Mozart's *Don Giovanni*. The Commendatore has a plan, and he carries it out in an ineluctable form. He may step down from his pedestal to complete it, but we have no doubt that once he is finished he will climb back up and remain there until the end of time.

Nothing like that happens in Ingmar Bergman's film *Cries and Whispers*, in which four female statues cry and whisper because they cannot accept the fact that life comes to an end. Amid fragmentary evocations of unbearable domestic secrets and obscure monologues, the entire movie revolves around a luminous shaft, the cone of light that unexpectedly falls on an eternal instant, on the sculptural group—a pietà—made up of maid and dying lady, the maid on whose bare bosom the dying lady rests. The fact that the lady was a painter opens the way to a curious maternal metaphor in which sculpture lovingly supports painting.

As I attempt to imagine what it is that sculptures cry or whisper, the reader may think I am allowing myself to be carried away by pure fiction. I will try to make myself understood by using another image, a photographic image of Auguste Rodin in his dilapidated studio at Meudon surrounded by a mass of white stones that perforce shine. Before being able to contemplate Constantin Brancusi's carved forest in his studio or Alberto Giacometti's figures of purulent plasticity in his, we must recognize that the imposing, prophetic effigy of Rodin, as it appears in the photograph, is that of the surviving patriarch after the deluge who raises his eyes for a moment from excavating remains, seeking out the fossils of life, listening perhaps to what the stones cry and whisper, like someone dreamily raising a seashell to his ear. Of this fragmented discourse there remains only a pile of shards.

Another real image, but one we must imagine—because, even as we lack the corresponding photographic evidence, what needs to be recorded are certain noises rather than sounds—is Degas's studio when Degas, almost blind, accumulated scores of wax figures, many of which were lost simply because they fell apart. Fragile by nature and not properly protected, they would burst, it seems, with any change of temperature or environmental shift. If we modify Degas's voyeuristic advice to spy on the body through the keyhole, we imagine ourselves carefully placing our ear against the studio door in an attempt to catch the noise these wax sculptures make when they disintegrate. With each muffled blow, each explosion, a chill. In contrast, the wax pieces by Medardo Rosso accumulate a pain that is without a doubt silent and will surprise us no matter what shelf they are placed upon.

With the pedestal lost, without the microphone at the podium, not everyone cries or whispers. Amid the confusion, there are some who choose to be silent, emphatically showing their silence, perhaps even making a gift of it. This introversion, this self-absorption, this digging into the interior in search of the peace of the abysmal night, the silence of intimacy, is not alien to the Western sculptural tradition, nor for that matter to the Western aesthetic tradition. The heart of the stone has been the objective of carvers, just as a mystical disinterest in forms seduced the Mannerists, who only wanted to be left with the pure *idea* or the pure *internal design*. But it is one thing to be silent and quite a different thing to enclose oneself within oneself. Aristide Maillol created a round silence where volumes enfold each other like the petals of a flower at nightfall. It is a silence of withdrawal, of immobility. It is a nontemporal silence, one with its own peculiar sound because it lacks intervals. It is, therefore, the opposite of what the Spanish writer José Bergamín described as "silent music," an allusion to the dancer's ecstasy that a bullfighter achieves in the supreme instant of his art. In Maillol's cosmic silence, there is no rhythm that creates, to say it in the words of another Spanish poet, John of the Cross, a "sonorous solitude." This silent, compact introversion, which reappears constantly throughout the century, although not in the same state of purity, is present in some Brancusi. It reappears in certain Minimalists.

Those who make "silent music" are those who draw in space—the Picasso of *Hommage à Apollinaire*, the late Julio González, Alexander Calder, the early Giacometti, David Smith. Their filamentous structures are musical instruments ready to vibrate, sometimes light and airy, like a subtle Japanese instrument, or with an empty space in them for resonance, like a Spanish guitar. In some works, these blacksmiths turn into noisy arms makers, hammering and beating.

I am not trying to construct a musical correlation of twentieth-century sculpture but to suggest some forms of attention that can help us penetrate secrets protected from our initial gaze. Our hearing organs not only enable us to perceive sounds but also to maintain our equilibrium and sense of orientation. By marking a path of truth and by revealing the truth of the journey, contemporary sculpture too has been concerned with orientation. We only hear our footsteps, but we leave very eloquent footprints, as, for instance, happens to and is documented by Richard Long.

The range of sonorous possibilities amplifies to infinity in our noisy urban centers, in which people and machines compete to make themselves understood. At what point do we put a limit on this game of metaphors, which can have no limit because metaphors link one to another? At the outset, I referred to the narrative ploy Guitry used to tell the history of France by means of a place, Versailles, filled with secrets piled up in its corners. Guitry's charm resides in his changes of humor, a bit like that practiced in the comic operas of Jacques Offenbach, who certainly knew how to direct our attention to the clay feet beneath all idols. Changes of humor are not reducible, speaking now about the avant-garde, to Marcel Duchamp's irony. The tragic dignity González succeeded in infusing into some of his welded figures or the comic pirouettes a few avant-garde Venuses twist themselves into can also offer unexpected comic arias or guffaws of metal. These changes of humor lead me to think about Offenbach or Guitry and not, for example, about "voices of silence," which, nevertheless, are also included in this history.

This, then, is a history or story that is far from over. To the contrary, it is in full swing. All first steps in technological innovation copy earlier models; the first automobiles imitated horse-drawn carriages, while today CD-ROMs pretend to be books. The sonorous affinities I have proposed include sculpture from the beginning and the end of this century. Probably, the crisis of the statue, the paradigm par excellence of classical sculpture, does not exhaust itself in the loss of the pedestal; instead, it generates another kind of eloquence. Three-dimensional pieces, even when they organize themselves spatially without taking the human body into account as a center, never cease to be monuments pregnant with nostalgia, musical airs whose sentimental resonance evokes other times. In reality, what is exciting about sculpture is that all of it is of the past and, therefore, unequivocally art. The present lacks plasticity and remains an inscrutable mystery.

At this *fin de siècle*, and with the availability of the formidable Nasher Collection, which contains almost all the musical instruments, the problem that arises is how to direct, how to harmonize, the orchestra. I have given a great deal of thought to the Guggenheim Museum, the enormous sculpture that is Frank Lloyd Wright's building, simultaneously an enchanted dream and a nightmare. Verticality and rings. The image of Dante's *Inferno* has also appeared in my dreams. Thus, the concentric journeys of two poets who hear different stories amid the cries and whispers. I have alluded to the cone of light made up, like a pietà, by maid and dying lady in the film *Cries and Whispers*. Images of Piranesi and William Blake also come to mind. Ultimately, there are always three elements: the spiral staircase, the loggia of busts speaking or singing tales, and the cone of light. I have used all of these to suggest a narrative, even if it is one barely heard.

In any case, my dreams cannot be told with words. They reside in the sculptures, which hide secrets. I dreamed about having the Nasher Collection at my disposal, about having a space like Frank Lloyd Wright's. I dreamed about being able to bring them together. In this dream, I walked through that concentric space, and it was occupied by a mountain of stories, a mountain of cries and whispers. I do not remember what I heard. When I awakened—this I do remember—I again recalled Guitry's film, perhaps in order to know that telling the secrets of history by walking through rooms in an old castle is not, after all, such a mad project.

Translated, from the Spanish, by Alfred Mac Adam.

Raymond Nasher, photographed in 1987 at the National Gallery of Art, Washington, D.C., with David Smith's *Voltri VI* (1962).

WHY SCULPTURE? AN INTERVIEW WITH RAYMOND NASHER. STEVEN A. NASH

This interview has been edited from conversations that took place on March 2 and 3, 1996 at the home of Raymond D. Nasher in Dallas. The Nasher home has long been a destination for museum professionals, artists, dealers, collectors, and others interested in Modern sculpture—all have been drawn not only by the extraordinary quality of the Patsy R. and Raymond D. Nasher Collection but also by one of the most aesthetically pleasing installations of sculpture to be found in a private setting. Anyone determined to acquire a full overview of the collection, however, must travel to numerous other sites as well, due to an effort to share aspects of this collection with a wider public through loans to not-for-profit and commercial venues alike. The interview focuses on the collection's history and the dynamics of opportunity and personal vision that shaped its growth; the importance of art in private lives and public consciousness; and the responsibilities that attend the stewardship of a major private collection. It should be noted that both Raymond and Patsy Nasher became my close personal friends during 1980–88, when I served as Deputy Director and Chief Curator at the Dallas Museum of Art.

Raymond Nasher was born in Boston in 1921, the only child of parents who consciously invested the time and effort to expose their son to the arts. A graduate of Boston Public Latin School, he received a Bachelor of Arts from Duke University. After four years of World War II service as a Lieutenant in the United States Navy, he returned to Boston and earned a Master of Arts in economics from Boston University. He has been awarded a Doctorate of Humane Letters from Southern Methodist University and has taught as a Visiting Fellow at Harvard Graduate School of Education, as well as lectured at Massachusetts Institute of Technology, Princeton University, Southern Methodist University, and University of Massachusetts.

Nasher's business career began with the planning of residential developments and expanded to include the building of industrial and office complexes and shopping centers. Environmental and aesthetic concerns ranked high in all of these projects. With NorthPark, for example, a shopping center opened in Dallas in 1965, Nasher worked with a team of architects and designers to create an environment that housed approximately two hundred retail stores and also provided handsome display spaces for sculpture and painting. As part of this complex, Nasher created NorthPark National Bank, which became the largest independent bank in Texas. He has merged this institution with

Comerica and now serves as Chairman of the Board of the Comerica Bank of Texas. He has regularly blended his interests in real estate development and banking with service in the public sector, with particular emphasis on urban and foreign affairs. He has held governmental appointments under Presidents Lyndon Johnson and George Bush.

Formation of the Nasher Collection resulted from a close partnership that started when Raymond met Patsy Rabinowitz, a native Dallasite who was attending Smith College. They married in 1949 and, the following year, moved to Dallas, where they raised three daughters, Andrea, Joan, and Nancy, each of whom now pursues an independent career and her own involvement in the arts. The building of their collection was a joint labor of love between husband and wife, and a major theme in their life together. Patsy Nasher passed away in 1988 after a long series of illnesses.

Assiduous collectors with widely varying interests, the Nashers bought prodigiously in four main areas: pre-Columbian and other ethnographic arts, including Guatemalan textiles; contemporary prints; Modern and contemporary painting; and Modern and contemporary sculpture. Donated to the Dallas Museum of Art in 1986, the Guatemalan textile collection is considered one of the finest of its kind in the country. The print collection, composed of approximately three hundred works, is also outstanding. The collection of sculpture now numbers over three hundred examples. The first large-scale survey of the sculpture holdings—entitled *A Century of Modern Sculpture: The Patsy and Raymond Nasher Collection*—appeared at the Dallas Museum of Art and the National Gallery of Art, Washington, D.C., in 1987–88; it subsequently traveled to Madrid, Florence, and Tel Aviv. The catalogue published on that occasion, which I edited, provides more information about the Nashers and extensive documentation of their collection at that time (Rizzoli, 1987). In the years since that exhibition and the death of Patsy Nasher, there have been changes in the original collection, with Raymond Nasher constantly striving to add important new works.—S.N.

Steven Nash: *Concerning the history of the Nasher Collection, one of your very first significant purchases of Modern art was a Ben Shahn painting.*

Raymond Nasher: Yes, that was *The Tennis Players* [n.d.], which I saw at Edith Halpert's Downtown Gallery in New York in the late fifties.

SN: *As your association with Halpert grew, there were quite a number of paintings you acquired, including works by Charles Sheeler, George L. K. Morris, and Stuart Davis. You really started more in the field of American Modernism.*

RN: Edith had a retinue of very important American artists she had supported during the depression. I had to go to New York frequently at that time, at the end of the fifties, and her gallery was on about Fifty-ninth or Sixtieth street. Edith was a great, great woman and was very dedicated to her artists, and fortunately—even though the prices seemed very high, in the hundreds up to a thousand dollars, which in those days was a lot of money—my wife and I were able to acquire some beautiful examples.

SN: *So Halpert's enthusiasm for Modern art was influential for you and your wife, Patsy, becoming serious collectors?*

RN: Yes, it really was. But I could go back a little bit to indicate that of course we really started collecting with pre-Columbian art. When we moved from Boston to Dallas in 1950, we determined that we would take our vacation in Mexico, never having been there, and that we would visit certain archaeological digs. We went to Chichén Itzá, Uxmal, Monte Albán, Tikal, Teotihuacán, and many of the places that were active archaeologically during that period, and we got to know many of the people involved. At that stage, superb pieces of pre-Columbian art could be bought in the ten, twenty, twenty-five dollar range.

SN: *You and Patsy put together a very significant collection of pre-Columbian art.*

RN: I think it had a great influence on us in relating to our love of sculpture.

SN: *You gave important examples to the Dallas Museum of Art, but much of the collection you still have at the house. Somewhat later there developed a special focus on Guatemalan textiles.*

RN: That was Patsy's beat, and it came out of our interest in Mayan and pre-Columbian culture. A couple of the textile dealers came through, and she took a very hard look and then started to study Guatemalan and what she called Mayan textiles. She really had a passion for them. In 1986, the Dallas Museum did a wonderful exhibition of our textiles, and is now planning a publication devoted to them.

SN: *When did an interest in ethnographic and archaeological objects and sculpture of ancient peoples begin to translate into a passion for Modern sculpture? What were your first acquisitions in the field of Modern sculpture?*

RN: I guess the first major acquisition was a birthday present that Patsy gave me, which was the Arp *Torso with Buds* [1961, p. 235]. Sidney Janis had it, and I think Patsy negotiated a deal with him for about $15,000, and she presented me with this sculpture. Of course, it's truly one of Arp's great works. The reason I keep it in the entryway to the house is symbolic in relationship to the fact that it was the first piece, and it also relates to nature seen outside through the glass windows, because of its theme of buds and organic growth. That Arp has such a wonderful feel; it's wonderful to touch. This is what can happen with sculpture as opposed to painting and one of the reasons that we were extremely interested in sculpture. It is something that you can feel. It is more animate than inanimate, and you become like friends, as opposed to a painting on the wall that you really can't go near.

SN: *You don't touch the painting for safety's sake, but it also represents a different world— you're looking through a window into a fictional world—whereas sculpture is something in your own space that is very real, as a physical, tactile presence. What is it about sculpture along those lines that speaks to you so loudly?*

RN: There is a sculpture's three-dimensionality on the one hand, and also the fact it's almost like an individual. Like a real person, you see it from different angles and perspectives, and you

Raymond and Patsy Nasher, 1965.

recognize it by different characteristic traits. It has so many personalities. One of the things I say once in a while, that gets under the skin of scholars, is that a great piece of sculpture is 360 different works, because I maintain that each degree of view of the sculpture, if it is done well, is a different composition. You get a different sensation from the work because you're seeing it in a different light, seeing different forms, noting how the interrelationships of light and form weave together and change. It's evolving, as opposed to the two-dimensional and static quality of painting. By the way, one other thing about sculpture that is very interesting when I think about "why sculpture?" is the different materials. I have counted thirty-nine different media in the Nasher Collection alone. So you get involved in the different processes and approaches.

SN: *I have found in my museum work that people have more trouble with sculpture than with painting. Perhaps this is partly due to the lack of color, but I think also that there is something slightly intimidating about it being out in their own space—which raises the whole issue of installation of sculpture. I know that for you part of the great joy of having a sculpture collection lies in the process of installation.*

RN: That's right, in the installation and physical work with the sculpture. It can be intimidating because it is totally different depending on how you place it. You read its form in regard to a particular position. It has a relationship with everything around it, with the interior or exterior elements and spaces that it relates to, whatever the environment is. And the placement of the work becomes a creative act that is part of that work. This is one reason that it was much more interesting for Patsy and me to move in that direction, the fact that when one deals with sculpture one almost has to become a lay artist. When I added on to the house in 1989–90 and reinstalled the collection, I spent three months placing all of these pieces. Every night, after work, I would have half a dozen people here and cranes and other equipment. Obviously, some of these objects weigh tons, but once they are placed, they may not work just right, and you have to move them, or you may have to adjust the angle or relate one work differently to another work. Also, you must determine the way the light is going to strike a sculpture, and the way that the nature around it changes with the seasons, so that you see it differently.

SN: *Working with all of these environmental issues in terms of installing the sculptures relates to more than just your domestic setting, doesn't it?*

RN: Historically, my major business was real estate development, planning, and building, and I had determined that I always wanted works of art in the buildings. Whether it was a residential or commercial project, shopping center, office building, whatever it might be, the sculpture was really much more solid and meaningful a part of the building than a painting would be.

SN: *Sculpture as an enhancement of everyday environment is a notion I'd like to return to in a bit in terms of your philosophy of living with art. Going back, however, to the formation of the*

Nasher house, living room, 1996.

Nasher Collection, after the Arp, which was quite a momentous beginning, what were some of the other early acquisitions?

RN: We happened to be in Milan in 1972 and there was a great exhibition of Calder stabiles at one of the galleries. *Three Bollards* [1970, pp. 196–97] was there and a half a dozen other huge pieces, and I was deeply interested in getting a major Calder stabile. I liked *Three Bollards*, which is black and arched, and Patsy loved a more star-shaped red and white piece that was huge and very interesting, but I didn't think it was as typical of Calder. We went back two or three times but didn't make a decision. We followed the exhibition to its next location at the Galerie Maeght on rue de Téhéran in Paris. However, when we got to the gallery, we suddenly saw in the courtyard the Miró *Moonbird* [1944–46; enlargement, 1966, cast 1967; p. 211]. It had just arrived, and I said to Patsy, "Oh my God!" Calder is great, but the *Moonbird* we felt was one of the most important works of Modern sculpture ever made. We inquired about it with the dealer, who said, "I thought you wanted to look at the Calders." And I said, "We may do that, too, but first let's look at this *Moonbird*." We did and decided to buy it, if I remember, for $50,000, which was a huge step up for us at the time. It really appealed to us because of that wonderful whimsical condition, with its wings and bulging eyes and horn. We knew we

Nasher house, living room, 1996.

might not have the same opportunity again. But then we said, "Where are the Calders?" The black *Three Bollards* and a few other Calders were all there in the gallery. We finally decided on *Three Bollards*, so it was quite a day of collecting!

SN: *The three works you have discussed, the Arp, the Miró, and the Calder, are all semiabstract but have a relationship to natural form, a kind of evocative quality of figuration about them, either in a surrealistic sense or through a reinterpretation of nature. I suppose Barbara Hepworth's* Squares with Two Circles (Monolith) *[1963, cast 1964, p. 249] would be one of the first fully abstract works you acquired.*

RN: It was, and we saw that in front of the Tate Gallery in London. We were with Peter Gimpel and his brother René, and together we came upon this fantastic, huge object standing in front of the Tate. It seemed so dynamic, with its tunneled circles and abutting plates, and it is actually two pieces of sculpture, since the back is shaped and patinated differently from the front. One of the Gimpels contacted Barbara Hepworth, who agreed to sell that piece to us and lend another work to the Tate.

SN: *There have been these two tracks, so to speak, in your collecting: there are the figurative or quasi-figurative works, by artists such as Moore, Miró, Matisse, and Giacometti; then there are* *those that are purely abstract, including works by Hepworth, David Smith, Tony Smith, and Mark di Suvero. Do you see these as mutually compatible interests? Have you ever had any preference toward abstraction or figuration?*

RN: Not from my point of view. Patsy was always extremely progressive in her interests because she was so deeply involved with the contemporary field. We both agreed that from the time of Rodin to today one had more revolutions in art history than from the time of Egyptian and Roman art to Rodin. If one looks at that hundred-year period, you just go down the line and go from the figurative tradition, coming from Michelangelo to Rodin, and then move into the explosion of different forms that came later. I felt that each different development was worth examining and that one shouldn't concentrate on just one element.

SN: *And this is what has made the twentieth century so intriguing for you personally, this idea of constant innovation and revolution?*

RN: That's the excitement of the twentieth century—the constant challenge of old ideas and the development of new ones. I want to be involved in some way with the new approaches as a part of the totality of the collection, because it is also a part of the totality of our own times, and I am just as interested in looking forward as backward.

SN: *It should be noted that you've always collected paintings, but the sculpture really is far and away the most important and most heavily cultivated side of the Nasher Collection, to the point where you have now over two hundred fifty pieces of sculpture.*

RN: It's now over three hundred.

SN: *Do you remember a conscious decision-making process that led you to concentrate on sculpture or did this focus evolve more gradually and naturally?*

RN: Patsy and I really decided quite consciously that we would continue to collect paintings and other things, but that our major concentration would be Modern sculpture, both contemporary and classic Modern. Patsy was more devoted to the contemporary, and I to early Modern. The decision to focus on sculpture had something to do with my business interests in real estate development and linking art with commercial projects. Also, sculpture cost less than paintings of comparable quality. A Matisse sculpture might be a tenth the price of a Matisse painting but could be every bit as good, if not better. And multiple casts gave sculpture greater availability. But mostly it was because we loved the physicality and presence of sculpture. Since we had five acres of land and some six hundred trees around our home, which provided an ideal setting for outdoor sculpture, we concentrated initially on very large pieces, and we found often that the larger the piece by a great artist, the less expensive it became because of the practical problems of dealing with it. So a disadvantage to other people became an advantage for us.

SN: *You mentioned that your tastes and interests tended to dovetail with those of your wife. I* *remember Patsy very well as a passionate, thoroughly dedicated collector who loved the pursuit of great works. Among her finest traits were her curiosity and her drive to find out everything she could about a particular work.*

RN: She was consumed by collecting and very intellectual, with great ability to do research. She in essence became a scholar. She got to know everyone in the field and really developed for us a great network of contacts. And she always did her homework, which is one reason we built such a good library on Modern sculpture. We often sought advice, as you know, but we always made up our own minds.

SN: *Did you always agree on your purchases?*

RN: We concluded that we would try to agree on every piece, but if we didn't, and one of us felt strongly, that person would still go after what they believed in. Duchamp-Villon is a case in point. Patsy didn't think that Duchamp-Villon was an especially important artist, whereas I happened to think that he was one of the greatest! A dealer friend of ours, Arnold Herstand, kept finding Duchamp-Villon sculptures, and I bought almost every one of them because I just thought he was wonderful. She totally disagreed but said, "If you like it, then that's what's really important."

SN: *Conversely, were there any contemporary works that you felt were just too hard to take?*

RN: Well, yes, the Jean-Michel Basquiats for example. I thought that one or two Basquiat paintings would be great because he was an interesting graffiti artist, but to have *twenty* was a little much! But Patsy thought he was worth it and kept acquiring and even traded with Andy Warhol for all kinds of other things. She really kept abreast of the contemporary market and went to New York regularly.

SN: *Please discuss further your tendency to collect certain key artists in depth, because that certainly is a salient characteristic of the collection as a whole. One thinks immediately of the deep holdings of Picasso, Matisse, Giacometti, Moore, David Smith, and others.*

RN: We made our first trip to Much Hadham, England, to visit Henry Moore at this studio in 1967. We were in London for the Wimbledon matches and learned that Moore was also a tennis fan, so we had that in common. At that time he was working on *Two Piece Reclining Figure No. 9* in plaster [the Nashers purchased a bronze of this piece in 1968, later deaccessioned]. We thought it was a great piece and wondered if, when he completed it, we might have the opportunity to buy it, because we wanted very much to have a major work by Moore in the collection. We got to like him very much. We even gave him some pre-Columbian art because of his interest in this field; he freely said he owed it a debt for its influence on his own work. In 1967, he also showed us the three pieces of stone he had found that he was hoping to work into a sculpture and that later that year, in fact, became the sources for the large bronze *Three Piece No. 3: Vertebrae* [1968, pp. 252–53]. I told him if he ever did make this work, to please let us know. We got a wire from him in 1968 saying that he had finished both pieces, that they were at the Tate Gallery in London in a retrospective, and that if we were interested we should come over and take a look at them and choose one. So we dashed over within the month and saw both pieces. Patsy liked *Reclining Figure No. 9*, and I liked *Vertebrae*, and for the first time Henry agreed to let a collector buy two pieces at once. It was a lot of money for us at the time, but really worth it. And then, as you know, we went on to buy numerous other Moore sculptures, including many maquettes. That was one instance of our collecting in depth.

SN: *So you were determined to have more than one example of certain artists that had particular appeal to you, or that you thought were distinctly varied in output or crucial to the history of Modern sculpture.*

RN: Yes. For example, when I became interested in Duchamp-Villon, I felt strongly that he was one of the key artists of the time, but not as well known as others. Of course, I fell in love with the *Large Horse* [1914; enlargement, fabricated 1966; p. 129], which is where it began.

SN: *Matisse has also been a particular focus of yours. One of your most recent acquisitions, in fact, is* Standing Nude, Arms on Head *[1906, p. 85], a lovely small Matisse.*

RN: With Matisse, we started with the *Large Seated Nude* [ca. 1925–29, p. 95], one of his greatest sculptures, which we bought in 1983. It was the most expensive work we ever bought up to that stage. It was more than twice the price of anything we had purchased before, and we had one day to make a decision on it. The dealer Heinz Berggruen brought it from Europe to New York. We had been looking at a cast of the same piece that had been offered to us at a much lower price, but, as it turned out, was not really available. It was a bogus deal. We went to see Berggruen's cast in New York and thought it was superb, and perfect in terms of conservation. But because there was supposedly so much interest in it, we'd have to make a decision that day. It was in the million-dollar range, which was a new threshold for us, but with some trepidation, Patsy placed a call, and we bought it. In a way, this work gave us the freedom and confidence to seek only the very best. It gave us a new sense of what was possible.

SN: *Then you acquired other Matisse bronzes in fairly rapid succession?*

RN: Yes. For example, in 1985, Sotheby's had both *Two Women* [1907, p. 91] and *Decorative Figure* [1908, cast early 1930s, p. 93] in the same auction. We went to see them and, as usual, tried to do as much research on them as possible. I determined that I especially liked the *Two Women*, and would be willing to make a special effort to acquire it. *Two Women* came before the *Decorative Figure* in the auction, and it just so happened that I was able to buy the *Two Women* for less than I had contemplated. So we had money left over and when the *Decorative*

Figure came up a little later, I said we should take a shot at it, and we were able to buy it as well. With the very rare plaster cast of *Madeleine I* [1901, cast 1903, p. 83], we were extremely lucky. The great dealer, Ernst Beyeler, had taken it in just before we paid him a visit in Basel. We were leaving his gallery to have lunch with him, and he remembered it almost as an afterthought. We saw it and bought it on the spot. A couple of years later, a member of the Matisse family told us they were very upset because they thought we might make bronze casts from the plaster, but we were able to put their minds totally to rest on that account.

SN: *Certainly, from the point of view of an art historian looking at the Nasher Collection, one of its great strengths is this representation of certain key artists through different creative moments and stylistic inventions. At some point in the development of the collection, did you begin to take a more scholarly perspective and, with the aim of making it a more complete survey, attempt to round it out historically?*

RN: Patsy always said that it was a strictly personal collection, and that we bought on instinct alone. But I would have to say that one does begin to get a sense of an historical whole and an awareness of gaps to be filled.

SN: *What are some of the works you have most desired for the collection but that, for one reason or another, have gotten away?*

RN: Patsy and I had wanted Picasso's *Monument to Apollinaire* [1928] which was available but involved certain questions about its date of manufacture, and by the time we did our research it was too late. We also missed Picasso's *Woman in the Garden* [1929–30], not once but *twice*, when it was first available ten years ago and again when it was offered last year at many times the original price. Matisse's *Serpentine* [1909] always eluded us. We never even saw it for sale. There are certain Brancusis that would be lovely to have, and that we looked at in the past, but he is one of the rarest artists of the century; and we always were particularly interested in Lipchitz's large and totemlike *Figure* of 1930. I think in the Picasso area we were very fortunate because the collection does have a range of Picasso sculptures and paintings that together reinforce one another and tell a great deal about Picasso the artist. The Picassos go from the Cubist period with the plaster *Head (Fernande)* [1909, p. 111] to one of his last large paintings, called *Nude Man and Woman* from 1971 [p. 327], which his wife Jacqueline told us was a premonition of his own death. Last year, I bid on a wonderful Modigliani stone head, which would have fit beautifully into the collection. It looked wonderful in the auction catalogue but turned out to be cracked through the neck, so I wasn't willing to pay the kind of price that it fetched.

SN: *That raises the issue of condition vis-à-vis sculpture. How does the condition of an object weigh in your mind when you're considering it for acquisition?*

NorthPark shopping center, Dallas, 1965.

RN: Sculptures in many ways are animate beings that are constantly changing, especially the outdoor pieces, and so, like people, they have to be given proper physical care; they have to be looked after and treated. The collection always presents a conservation problem; not a problem but a responsibility. Some pieces, for example, have to be repainted; some require new patinas. Outdoor works need to be cleaned and sometimes waxed. But it is necessary to do the proper research to determine the correct treatment and the correct materials. To neglect an outdoor sculpture is the same as destroying a work of art. For the collection, we have always kept up a program of inspection and maintenance. It is part of living with the works, but it does make ownership more complicated. We have worked directly, for example, with Tony Caro, the Henry Moore Foundation, and the Dubuffet Foundation to determine proper methods for treating works.

SN: *It represents a level of responsibility and expense that perhaps discourages in general the collecting of large outdoor works. Earlier you mentioned your visits with Henry Moore, which I know were a source of great pleasure for you. And Moore visited you in Dallas, where he made a beautiful drawing of one of your Oceanic sculptures. Are there any other experiences with artists that you recall as particularly memorable?*

RN: We have had many wonderful moments with artists. We gave a party once for Andy Warhol. Andy traveled usually with fifteen or twenty people, and we didn't realize it at the time, but he rarely said a word. Patsy had a natural rapport with artists, though, and she persuaded him to make portraits of her and our three daughters. And we had another party for Frank Stella that I'll never forget, mostly because Frank was so tough and even abrasive. But we got to know him, visited him a dozen times, went to his studio, and developed a great respect for him and also his scholarship. Lichtenstein is a delight to know, as well as Oldenburg and Shapiro and many other artists in the collection. Knowing them adds a dimension to their work.

SN: *You worked with Richard Serra on different occasions. How did that go?*

RN: Richard came and set up the *Inverted House of Cards* [1969–70, p. 261] here in the garden, and later we bought the huge *My Curves Are Not Mad* [1987, pp. 262–63] in Brooklyn, and he came down to install it in front of the Dallas Museum of Art. That was quite an operation. It was 110 degrees outside, and it was complicated work, positioning two giant steel plates in

NorthPark shopping center, Dallas, 1965.

extremely precise alignment. I was greatly impressed with Richard's painstaking exactitude and his engineering skills. It was during that visit that Serra found out I had just had a meeting with Gorbachev. He had invited me to Moscow because he and Raisa had seen the collection at the National Gallery of Art in Washington, and they wanted to discuss a tour of the collection to Moscow and Leningrad. Serra is from a Russian background, and he said, "If the collection goes there, I'll carry your bags, I'll do anything to go there." So I asked him, "Well, would you create a piece of sculpture in a factory in Moscow?" I'd talked to Raisa about doing that because I thought it would be fabulous for Serra to do one of his large steel pieces there, and he said it would be his greatest joy; he'd even do it "on the house." [Neither the tour nor the sculpture came to fruition.] He is a fascinating man, an individualist.

SN: *Didn't Ellsworth Kelly, at the time of the first exhibition of the Nasher Collection in 1987, make a special work for your consideration?*

RN: Not exactly. You and your colleagues at the Dallas Museum of Art had commissioned a sculpture from Kelly for the new museum when it opened in 1984. He came to visit the museum and saw our collection when it was exhibited there in 1987. We spoke at that time, and I said we had a great Kelly painting in *Block Island II* [1960] but hadn't found just the right sculpture. He thought there was one that would be perfect for the exhibition, but it was out in Los Angeles. I was headed to New York, however, so he had it shipped East. It was the first piece that he had done without a base, so the work [*Untitled*, 1986, p. 313] seems to rise straight out of the ground without any support—very elegant and sleek [the support is hidden in the ground]. We acquired it and sent it to join the exhibition at its second stop, at the National Gallery. But there was a big to-do with the trustees at the National Gallery because in order to install the work they would have to cut into their new marble floors. It required a special trustees' meeting and decision to permit its installation.

SN: *We have been talking about the history of the collection, but perhaps we could shift focus now to the philosophy behind it. I've always found revealing your ideas about the social role of art and the connections in your own life between art and public purpose. You are best known as a real estate developer and banker, but you also have a long history of work in the public and governmental sectors. Perhaps you could sketch for us some of those involvements.*

RN: In government, I first started work when I was asked by Lyndon Johnson to run the White House Conference on International Cooperation, which led to the publication in 1965 of a major book entitled *Blueprint for Peace*. During 1964–65, I chaired the National Commission on Urban Development and later was involved in creating the Department of Housing and Urban Development, making it a Cabinet position. In 1967–68, I served in an ambassadorial position as a representative to the General Assembly of the United Nations. Later, I taught at Harvard for three years at the Graduate School of Education and have maintained my interests in the Council on Foreign Relations and the American Assembly. To keep this brief, I haven't mentioned some other government and teaching positions.

SN: *Do you feel that these involvements in public service have influenced your notions about public art?*

RN: They have made me more aware of the social and educational functions of art. It is vitally important aesthetically because it improves the whole nature of the environment of whatever project or space is involved. But it also is a matter of attitudes, the attitudes of employees, visitors, customers, whoever. For example, I'm a great believer that from an aesthetic and an environmental point of view, employees enjoy much greater productivity in an environment in which art plays a major function. I've been able to test that theory in my bank and shopping center. When there is an exhibition and lots of art around, you find a mental relationship which relates to productivity and activity and, in general, a better human relationship between people. There is also an educational factor. Major works from the collection are constantly shown at NorthPark shopping center, and for many people, it is their first exposure to art. You have to realize that more people will see great art within the shopping center in a month than will see it in our city museums within the year, which may be unfortunate but true. The exposure of people to the arts within commercial spaces gets them extremely interested, and they'll come back with family and friends. Exposure is crucial. People may look at the art in this commercial space and totally shake their heads and reject it because they don't understand it or think it's irrational. But often you will see them come back, talk about a Henry Moore or a Jim Dine or a Jonathan Borofsky, and learn something about the nature of art.

SN: *It's a seed that is planted, and you hope that it grows.*

RN: Which I think is a great contribution. From a social point of view, one of the primary ingredients of life involves the human aspect of art. If you're interested in art, you look at the world around you and see things differently, with clearer eyes and greater sensitivity. I also think it helps you understand people better. Art used to be a primary part of our education system, and it has been practically eliminated. It is mandatory now with our highly technological society that we bring this exposure back to people.

SN: *Along these lines, you have always said that you don't like to have any art in storage. Is the idea of public access to your collection a key consideration?*

RN: Yes. I'm concerned that ninety percent of the art that's owned by museums and other institutions is not seen. My feeling is that these resources have to be shared. There are so many cities, towns, villages, universities, schools, and public places that have little or no art available. As far as the Nasher Collection is concerned, it is either used at home, installed in office buildings, shopping centers, or banks, or on loan to other institutions, universities, city buildings, or schools. I want to see the art becoming a fundamental catalyst in people's lives. It's a sharing process.

SN: *On the private, domestic side, you have created a stunning environment of art, architecture, and nature at your home. And you recently improved matters further by acquiring more land for outdoor sculpture and adding library and gallery spaces onto the house. You clearly place a high priority on these daily surroundings and being surrounded by great art.*

RN: It is fundamental to my whole outlook on life. The artworks are like friends that I greet every day. When they go off on loan, it is like being away from a family member. Our thesis was that Patsy and I wanted to have our children and ourselves exposed to intellectually and visually interesting objects. Rather than doing other things, we would fill our life with art.

SN: *Yet, it could be said that not all the objects are easy to live with. Some are challenging and stimulating and even upsetting. Which stand out for you in this way?*

RN: The Picasso painting *Nude Man and Woman* is a good example. When we first bought it in 1982, this work upset many people due to the nudity, the challenging masklike faces, and Picasso's almost ferocious expressiveness. As I said before, when Jacqueline Picasso saw it here she said it was a premonition of Picasso's death. It's a tough, hard piece, but intellectually it is tremendously stimulating. Each work in itself is one that we felt we wanted to live with and have as a part of a lasting friendship. The Gauguin wooden sculpture, *Tahitian Girl* [ca. 1896, p. 81], is another troubling piece—beautiful in the smooth, gentle carving of the face, but odd and wondrous in the unbalanced proportions of the body and the awkward stance. But this is what makes it so interesting to look at every day. And you certainly wouldn't say the Richard Serra *Inverted House of Cards* is a beautiful object. It is minimal and rusty and a little dangerous. It's a piece of engineering. Its steel plates fold in on each other, defying gravity and creating a unique, singular experience. Mark di Suvero's work strikes me in the same tough, exciting way. And think of Picasso's *Head of a Woman* from 1931 [cast 1973, pp. 112–13]. This is an extremely sexual work. When people finally catch on to it, they sometimes gasp. But that's great, because it really makes them think and respond. We didn't want just polite works around us.

Nasher house, back terrace, 1996.

SN: *It's perhaps impossible with a collection this large to single out any particular favorites, but sometimes a parent has favorite children, and I wonder, having lived with the collection all these years, if there are a few pieces that especially stand out in your mind.*

RN: When you have three girls as I do, you can't have a favorite. As for the art itself, there are probably a few pieces that mean the most to me, but for very different reasons. Seeing Henry Moore create *Three Piece No. 3: Vertebrae* and knowing the man so well give that work for me a special dimension. Miró's *Moonbird* is a piece that always makes you smile. He had a great sense of humor, and it is depicted in the *Moonbird*, where he's kind of laughing at the world and at the same time indicating a deep, mythical feeling about primitive or alien forms of life or what a bird might be like on the moon. I love Brancusi's *The Kiss* [1907–08, cast before 1914, p. 107]; he took a stone block and was able to bring warmth, love, beauty, and passion to it by utilizing his tools to carve it in a way that might seem very simple but actually is very eloquent. Giacometti's three busts of his brother Diego are favorites, partly because of the way he combined modeling and painting so beautifully [see pp. 156–57, 159, 161]. Maybe the fact that we knew Diego well also helps. A very different work is Barnett Newman's *Here III* [1965–66, p. 251]. It is difficult for many people to understand. They find it a little cold, too conceptual. But it is amazing to me how Newman got such spirituality out of such minimal

Nasher house, garden, 1996.

metallic form. Among the many Matisses, it would be hard to choose, but I think my personal favorite is the early *Reclining Nude (I) Aurora* from 1906–07 [p. 87]. It is very powerful for a relatively small-scale sculpture, and shows how Matisse manipulated parts of the body to compose them like a musical score.

SN: *You have been discussing mostly historical examples, but the collection is strong also on the contemporary side. With a collection as big as this, do you feel the need or the desire to continue moving it into newer developments by acquiring works by younger artists?*

RN: Yes, definitely. It's mandatory to continue, and one has to keep abreast of younger movements. I'm always considering possible additions and am interested, for example, in some of the new things going on in England today. One of my most recent acquisitions is the full-scale plaster of Rodin's great *The Age of Bronze* from circa 1876 [p. 61], which came from the Rudier family in France, famous for running the foundry that made so many of Rodin's casts. But on the contemporary front, I also acquired Magdalena Abakanowicz's *Bronze Crowd* of thirty-six life-size figures from 1990–91 [pp. 314–15]. I had originally seen them at the Walker Art Center in Minneapolis at the opening of the sculpture garden. I just thought they were incredible. They had a tremendous amount of depth, pathos, and the sense of uncertainty on the one hand as to what the future would be for these people, and resolute strength on the other hand, conveyed by their erect stance. They seem so symbolic of a great deal that is happening in the world today.

SN: *It's interesting that two of your most recent acquisitions span the full breadth of your sculpture collection, from Rodin in the 1870s to Abakanowicz in the 1990s. This is characteristic of the broad range of ideas and tastes and historical coverage that are represented within the collection. But I would think that changes in the market for Modern sculpture make it continually more difficult to expand that coverage. What are the main differences between collecting now and collecting fifteen or twenty years ago?*

RN: Well, there are the obvious changes in prices and availability. Fifteen, twenty-five years ago there was the ability, in sculpture, to find amazing masterworks, partly because sculpture was relatively less popular than painting at that time, and some works were still available in multiple casts. Now the flow of great works has slowed to a trickle, and the prices reflect this scarcity. Also, there is now greater competition for fewer works. You can still find things—just last year I was able to buy Medardo Rosso's *Jewish Child* [ca. 1892–93, cast 1900–14, p. 77] and Gauguin's clay *Torso of a Woman* [ca. 1896, p. 79] at auction for very favorable prices, because others overlooked them—but it takes work.

SN: *Has it become less fun?*

RN: Today? It may be less fun because I know more about it than I did then. At that early stage, our emotions were as deeply involved as our intellect. Often when Patsy and I saw something exciting, we became very emotionally involved and would say, "We *have* to have this; this is something that will *never* come again in our lifetime." And I'm glad we did get so involved. Now, I'm more discerning, more choosy, and also more picky about the quality of the cast or the whole issue of condition. Nevertheless, it still is exciting. There's nothing like the discovery, the chase, and the capture. The pursuit of the Rodin *The Age of Bronze* was a tremendously exciting experience. I spent many days just tracking it down, doing the research, comparing the plaster to bronze casts, negotiating, jockeying with a neighboring museum that also wanted it, thinking it was gone but finally achieving it. It was great!

SN: *Would you agree that there is a certain fashionability to collecting contemporary art that makes older works such as the Rodin plaster more attractive in terms of prices?*

RN: Yes, it's a matter of marketing and all the galleries and press and socializing devoted to contemporary art. Works like the Rodin or Rosso's *Jewish Child* are bargains compared to works that you see at auctions of contemporary art. But it's a question of what interests you the most.

SN: *Do you have any particular advice for young collectors who are just getting started?*

RN: Education is the key. Go to museums and galleries as much as possible, and read as much

Nasher house, garden, 1996.

as possible. Get a feeling for what attracts you personally the most. And, then, the key issue is to be a risk taker; most people who want to collect art never do because they can't make a decision about quality, and they also worry about the opinion of other people. Risk taking also means being willing to put down the funds once you make up your mind.

SN: *So, find something that you really love, and be willing to take a risk intellectually and financially. What about the notion of art as an investment?*

RN: That's a totally different business; nothing that we bought was bought as an investment. We bought because we wanted the object and without ever thinking about whether it would appreciate or depreciate in value. When you're buying art as an investment, you're in a different business. Art really is about love. It's something you want to live with, look at, touch, expose people to. And if you're looking at it as a stock or a bond, then you are just relating to the marketplace. You may as well go into the gallery business.

SN: *We have talked a lot about the history of the collection, and your philosophies of collecting, but what about the future? What would be an ideal scenario for the future of the collection?*

RN: One important aspect is to continue to acquire, to make the collection better and keep it current, fresh, and alive. The second consideration is to determine how it can serve the greatest purpose in the future. It would lose its meaning if it were split into pieces. My feeling is that it should remain together, that it be part of a private museum run by my foundation, relating to this house and perhaps additional land, where it could be seen by appointment in the present environment, which is so wonderful. Or another approach would be to work with a public museum and fold it into a museum setting where it could remain intact and contribute to the quality and nature of that particular museum. In either case, I am thinking about the educational potential of a new institute of Modern sculpture that would focus study and research on the collection but would also embrace the whole subject of Modern sculpture. With the museum and collection would come the scholarship leading to publications, catalogue raisonnés, exhibitions, seminars, and lectures. If all these things were tied together, the collection would be the center of a larger reality that would truly serve posterity. The Nasher Collection is a representation of revolutionary ideas in sculpture, and I am now talking about a revolutionary idea in how sculpture is studied, involving new technologies and a great research library, an international network of scholars and museums, and an ambitious program of exhibitions and services. May as well think big!

INSIGHT AND FORM. MICHAEL BRENSON

This has been a magical century for sculpture. Whether building on approaches to carving or modeling developed over centuries, or exploring new or found materials, or taking their leads from the conceptual and gestural freedom of painting or from the inventiveness and urgency of art from other cultures, Modernist sculptors have done as much as any other artists to deepen and transform the ability of art audiences to feel and to think. They have been instrumental in redefining nature, reshaping the body, reimagining time and space. They have reinstilled in Western sculpture a sense of mystery and nerve. They have given it, once again, a soul.

The Patsy R. and Raymond D. Nasher Collection makes it possible to take stock of what Modernist sculptors have achieved. The collection includes exceptional works by so many pioneering figures—including Constantin Brancusi, the remarkable and still underknown Raymond Duchamp-Villon, Naum Gabo, Alberto Giacometti, Henri Matisse, Pablo Picasso, Auguste Rodin, Medardo Rosso, and David Smith—that it almost obliges viewers to ask questions that need to be asked now, at the end of the Modernist era, when the meanings and legacies of Modernism are more contested than ever. What has Modern sculpture meant to art? What has it meant to culture? How successful has it been in offering the kinds of experiences that will help future generations understand what it meant to be alive in a century in which responses to the mundane and the cosmic may have changed more than in all the previous centuries combined?

This essay suggests the character and scope of Modernist sculpture through a discussion of selected works in the Nasher Collection.[1] Although an essay on Modern sculpture confined to one private collection is, by definition, incomplete, the Nasher Collection touches so many bases and its strengths are so deep that it encourages broad insights and meditations. More than any other collection of twentieth-century sculpture in private hands, it inspires speculation on what makes Modernist sculpture modern and why any given sculpture demands attention.

By discussing works in this collection in terms of interior and exterior, balance, pressure, and enchantment, I hope to encourage people to think once again about the language of sculpture. It has been by exploring issues of surface, light, shape, volume, balance, size, scale, solid, and void that sculptors throughout the century have found ways to be equal to the challenges of their times. Through investigations of sculpture's language, they have been able to rethink movement, assert or defy gravity, feel the texture and shape of space, and transform trauma into hope.

The sculptural issues explored by the artists in the Nasher Collection cannot be exhausted. It is equally clear that talking about these issues exclusively, or even primarily, in formal or ideological terms can never be enough. What many of these sculptors accomplished is generous and moving. It is only by being sensitive to the courage and poetry of their struggles, and by suggesting the ways in which their explorations touch feelings and thoughts basic to many people, that Modernist sculpture can be effectively gauged. If the Nasher Collection is approached with a sense of curiosity and discovery, it will be clear that far from being an overcultivated, overanalyzed, overfamiliar field, Modernist sculpture is still largely unknown.

Interior and Exterior

Auguste Rodin's *The Age of Bronze* (ca. 1876, p. 61) is the earliest work in this exhibition and one of the most influential works in the collection. A youthful male nude stands alone. His left leg is firmly planted; his right leg is bent at the knee, as if beginning to move. His mouth is slightly open; his eyes are closed. His flesh and muscle were modeled with extraordinary gentleness and concentration. Because of the intimate attention to every inch of the surface, the skin draws light to itself. Light is able to caress the body, enveloping it in a welcoming glow. Flesh and muscle are extolled. The nude body—the mechanics and indeed the substance of physical being—has been treated with such reverence as to seem almost holy.

This figure, however, is like two radically different figures. While the right hand grips the head by the hair, the left hand is in the process of opening. Although the rest of the body is that of an idealized young man, the physiognomy of the face is less idealized, perhaps suggesting a man of labor. Just as important, the man's mental and spiritual life is far less finished than his body; it is not so much youthful as unformed, in the process of being born. It is as if his inner life—tentative, uncertain, even vulnerable—has been set in motion toward creation, toward the world, toward the sky. The mouth is open just enough to allow an utterance to begin to emerge. Since it is still sealed inside the body, however, we cannot know what that utterance, or what this youth's inner life, is.[2] While the exterior of the body is so tactile that it seems within our grasp, the interior is so private as to be inaccessible.

The same sense of two separate realities, one public, the other private, is suggested by Rodin's *Study for the Monument to Balzac* (ca. 1897, cast 1974, p. 65). The physical presence of Honoré de Balzac, the nineteenth-century literary giant on whose sculpture Rodin worked during a five-year period, is overwhelming. The bulk is so imposing and the body so organic in its outgoing energy that Balzac seems like a force of nature. The strong features of the face and the manelike hair suggest a man who declared his place in the world with great physical authority, and whose irrepressible creativity was inseparable from his physical command. Balzac's body, although robed, seems as majestically responsive to air and light as a great oak and as immovable as a cliff.

But in this sculpture, too, Rodin evoked an interior and exterior in conflict. The face looks bruised and pained, suggesting a psychological and emotional life far more anxious than the immovable body would imply. The indentation of the right cheekbone and the shadows under the eyes suggest sleeplessness. With his nocturnal inner life, Balzac is revealed as a man who carried feelings within himself that he struggled with bitterly and that he did not want anyone to see. This is a cultural hero who understands the meaning of psychic damage. His physical authority—the straightforward, even exhibitionistic, force of his body—suggests someone all of a piece but who could not be whole. Rodin's Balzac is right there, fully present, in our space, but we cannot possess him. His psychological and imaginative life belongs to him alone.

Through works like these, Rodin helped bring into sculpture new ways of dealing with modern life, whose conflictual nature could not be effectively explored in any sculptural aesthetic that advocated the unified expression of a feeling, attitude, or idea. For example, after Rodin's responsiveness to both an exterior and an interior self, each with a distinct identity, it was easier for artists to think creatively about a world of hype and spectacle in which the public face of a man or woman could differ radically from the private one—and in which a need for the spotlight could coexist with a longing for a world of shadows in which there is no threat of invasion. It was also easier for artists to build into their work the impact of a societal collision between power and powerlessness, and sometimes the experience of both within the same person.

One of the few contemporary sculptors Rodin admired was Medardo Rosso. In the heads that Rosso began modeling in wax a few years after *The Age of Bronze*, there is both a will to exposure and a wariness of being exposed. Like many of Rodin's sculptures, Rosso's waxes are tactile, eliciting a desire to touch, and sensitive to light. The mass often seems to be enveloped by a blast of light that floods the face, stripping all detail from it, leaving it naked. But as in

Impressionist painting, the more palpable light becomes, the more it conceals as much as reveals. In sculptures like *The Concierge* (ca. 1883–84, p. 71) and *Sick Child* (1889, p. 75), the envelope of light covers the head with a film or veil that seals off the inner life of the woman or child. The same light that brings the figure to life in the present also has an embalming effect that preserves and memorializes. In Rosso's sculptures, the tension between directness and secretness, nakedness and privacy, can be almost excruciating in its suggestion of a self at once brimming with confidence and in danger.

In the sculpture of Brancusi, exposure and secrecy, lack of inhibition and restraint, become compatible. In *Bust of a Boy* (1906, p. 105), one of Brancusi's earliest surviving sculptures, the nakedness and exposure communicate both a will to openness and a profound sense of vulnerability whose coexistence is healing. Few of Brancusi's works encourage clear connections between his aesthetic and his life, but this one recalls the traumatic treatment Brancusi received from his father and brothers, which led him to run away from home at the age of eleven. *Bust of a Boy* suggests an injury that needs to be both revealed and healed—revealed in order to be healed.[3] The agent of transformation is light. In *Nancy Cunard (Sophisticated Young Lady)* (1925–27, p. 109), Brancusi's particular sculptural combination of extroversion and introversion results in a more worldly and witty statement. The curve of the belly throws itself into the space around it, eager for contact with the world, but the body is held back by the diagonal, corkscrew handle-like chignon, which shifts the weight toward the rigid and self-contained vertical. And because of the seamlessly polished surface of the wood, the interior reality of the same stylish mass that projects itself into the light is present but coyly inaccessible. In Brancusi's work, the startling equilibrium between exposed, down-to-earth, simple exterior and elusive interior, between gregariousness and privacy, helps to define an attitude that became useful to many later sculptors, including the Minimalists. That attitude is very much: Here the sculpture is, all there, right in front of you, with nothing to hide; it wants you, just as it wants light and space, but it is also restrained and secretive, and wherever you might think it is, it is always someplace else.

The interrelationship between projection and protection continued to shape figurative as well as abstract sculpture after World War II. In George Segal's *Rush Hour* (1983, cast 1985–86, pp. 296–97), which clearly comes out of and comments on Rodin's heroic groups, six ordinary men and women stride forward, absorbed in the kind of blind movement that defines their commuter lives. They have that see-nothing-hear-nothing look commuters get after too many rush hours. They are going where they have to but not thinking about it, not interested anymore in the space they plow through, simply trying to get through it. Their physical realities are forceful and assertive, and Segal's sculptures are so tactile that they almost ask to be touched, but their inner selves are so private they appear to be riddles to everyone looking at them and also to themselves. Like Rosso's heads, they seem to have veils or films over their faces so that whatever is going on inside them is unreachable. The division between the forcefulness and tactility of their bodies and movements and the inaccessibility of their inner selves is a reflection of their alienated lives.

In *The Age of Bronze* and *Monument to Balzac*, this division was a discovery. In Rodin's work, protecting or releasing the interior was a matter of choice. For Balzac, as Rodin saw him, this protectiveness was a conscious and necessary act. In *Rush Hour*, however, the separation of the inner self from its bodily existence is a sign not of possibility, of exercising will, but of disassociation. And, to a degree that could not be predicted from Rodin's sculpture, it has also become a sign of exile. Rodin's figures clearly belong to themselves. They have the ability to make a place for themselves in the world. Segal's figures do not. It is not just that they are involved in numbingly repetitive daily movements. They seem cast adrift without boat or captain. The split between their physical movements and their inner selves reflects a homelessness that has become a permanent condition.

In the *Bronze Crowd* (1990–91, pp. 314–15) by the Polish artist Magdalena Abakanowicz, whose work has also been influenced by Rodin, the tension between interior and exterior has an altogether different meaning. Poland had only recently freed itself of the Communist regime that ruled there for over forty years. In Communist Poland, where political power was absolute and obedience demanded, the imagination and intellect—aspects of inner life—were just about the only sources of refuge and freedom. Abakanowicz's thirty-six standing nude figures, hiding nothing, totally exposed, give an impression of complete obedience. Cast from burlap, the fronts of their bodies are wrinkled. Their skins, or hides, are maps of age and time, emblems of the exploitation and servitude they endured. They stand like soldiers or workers at attention, their headless bodies waiting for orders.

From the back, however, the figures are radically different. They are not fully rounded but hollow, like half-shells. Cast from styrofoam, the inner linings are smooth, offering places in which viewers can shelter themselves from the world to which the fronts of the figures are so exposed. The interiors are not only sources of protection but, as is so often the case in Abakanowicz's work, they carry within them the hint of cocoons or nests. They bring into the work the possibility of newness and the suggestion of a reality that may have nothing in common with the flesh-and-blood realities branded on the flesh. Although the interiors are empty, they seem alive and welcoming—as if souls have been there, or may even be there still.

In *The Age of Bronze*, Rodin brought into sculpture the hallowed presence of that which is on the verge of being born, and which, when born, is capable of becoming something not yet imagined. This presence helped shape the entire organic sculptural tradition that runs through the work of Brancusi, Jean Arp, and Henry Moore, and it finds one of its most eloquent manifestations in the interiors of Abakanowicz's sculptural bodies.[4] The Modernist fascination with the idea of new life, beginning to surge, capable in principle of transforming the world, continues to inform many kinds of art that appear to have little or no relation to Modernism. Finding a forceful poetic language in which to communicate the irresistible force of the new is a challenge that will continue to inspire artists well into the next century.

Balance

The single most mesmerizing gesture in Modernist sculpture may be the backward tilt in Rodin's *Monument to Balzac*. By tipping the massive body off axis, Rodin found a way to communicate several ideas at once. He suggested that Balzac's personality was defined by reserve and by a strong and very particular sense of irregularity and difference. Also, in the way the diagonal line of the back rises out of the short reverse diagonal connecting the figure to the base, and out of the short swell just above it, Rodin suggested suppleness and spring, making it seem as if this prolific writer was governed by laws as appropriate to plants and trees as they were to human nature.[5] With an imbalance that seems comfortable and logical but that is, in fact, extraordinarily awkward if not anatomically impossible, Rodin made a case for a notion of sculptural truth determined by the sculptural imagination. After *Monument to Balzac*, the body could be what the sculptor believed it had to be to serve a feeling or a thought. For Rodin, formal discovery and excitement always served content, but his formal insights were so free, original, and unexpected that the exploration of form inevitably became a source of sculptural interest in itself.

Of the early Modernists to build on the inventiveness of Rodin, one of the most important was Henri Matisse. In his *Large Seated Nude* (ca. 1925–29, p. 95), a naked woman is sitting near one edge of a squat, rounded block. Her arms (bent in the V-shape that Rodin, inspired by Michelangelo, used in the right arm of *The Age of Bronze*), torso, and head lean back, stretching the body into space. The legs pull the figure in the opposite direction. The left foot is tucked under the right thigh so that only the ball of the right foot connects the figure to the ground. If the balance is, in naturalistic terms, highly unlikely, if not impossible, so is the elongated and eccentrically proportioned body. But the imbalance seems appropriate to the nature of the figure, and the sculpture feels right. One reason for its success is Matisse's mastery of light. By modeling sculptural volumes that react to light as if dancing with it, Matisse made it possible for each segment to assert its reality and for the different parts of the body to be composed in space like forms in a painting. The work also has conviction because of Matisse's treatment of the stomach musculature and the segmented torso. The stomach musculature—which holds the center of gravity in the belly and hips, at the point where the buttocks are attached to a cushionlike block—suggests a performer, perhaps an acrobat or dancer, an association of athleticism strengthened by the sit-up position of the arms and elbows. The segmented torso creates the impression that the belly and chest are capable at any moment of folding in over the hips and therefore, if necessary, moving into balance.

In early Modernist sculpture, balance had become an issue, and when it did, the consequences were enormous. If sculpture did not have to be true anymore to naturalism but rather to sculptural logic, then it had a new kind of experimental and conceptual freedom. By reaching a fresh understanding of the language that made this logic possible, sculptors could suggest that the body was capable of almost unlimited expressiveness and movement, and that, like sculpture itself, it could be a laboratory of experimentation.

The issue of balance raised essential questions. What does it mean, really, to be physically and emotionally balanced? What does it mean to struggle to get one's balance? Isn't imbalance, as well as balance, a viable, if not a natural, condition? Doesn't the consciousness of imbalance bring with it an awareness of feelings and thoughts that are potentially creative once they are no longer hidden?

Most of the inventive explorations of balance have been made by abstract sculptors. Balance was an important issue for David Smith, who learned essential lessons about balancing acts in space from Julio González's sculpture and found in disequilibrium a truth of modern life and a principle of modern beauty. Smith's *9/15/53* (1953, p. 183), is composed around a short vertical neck that tilts to one side, then the other. On top of it, to one side, Smith welded a long horizontal strip of steel. Extending the horizontal in the opposite direction is a shorter and thicker strip. Projecting from the top of the longer horizontal are seven abstract forms, each a few inches tall, perched like birds on the limb of a tree. On the shorter and thicker strip are eight abstract forms, far more varied in size and shape, three of which appear to be impaled. The basic vertical and horizontal structure suggests a seesaw or scale, but the asymmetry and disorder within this structure of balance is as wild and unruly as a group of children whose parents have just left them unattended. This drama of disequilibrium has that rawness, intimacy, and defiance that Smith brought to the character of American sculpture.

Balance was an essential issue for many of the sculptors whose work came out of Smith's. In the 1960s and 1970s, Anthony Caro challenged existing conventions of sculptural equilibrium so consistently that his challenge to conventional notions of balance seems almost systematic. In his *Carriage* (1966, pp. 238–39), the relationships between the rectangular mesh screens and rectangular steel beams facing each other across a thirteen-foot space continually thwart expectations. The two eccentric points at which a round steel tube, half on and half off the floor, is attached to the beams, the way the mesh extends slightly beyond the edges of two other beams, the way a vertical beam is turned off axis, all undermine the initial sense of predictability and transparency produced by the geometric and transparent forms. In the end, the transparent mesh looks more impenetrable than the solid beams, and the round strip of steel tubing on the floor carries more formal weight than the thicker beams, including those with a columnar verticality. At his best, Caro could make up seem down, open seem closed, and gravity seem weightless. And he could go as far as Smith in rejecting the "monolithic limit in the tradition of sculpture" and arguing that sculpture "is as free as the mind."[6]

Mark di Suvero has worked with steel in a more improvisational and physical manner than Caro has. Di Suvero's *In the Bushes* (1970–75, p. 269) is a roughly twelve-foot-tall and ten-foot-wide construction of steel I-beams tipped so much to one side that it looks as if it has to fall, as if it has to lose its footing. The angle at which the sculpture is bent over brings to mind shipwrecks. The I-beams carry the kind of heroic emotional impact associated with Abstract Expressionism and the painter with whose work di Suvero's sculpture is often identified, Franz Kline. In di Suvero's work, however, there is also a raucous and high-spirited quality to the arrangement of beams that suggests children trying to push one another off a dock. The physical imbalance reinforces the imbalance between the playfulness and gravity of the content. In sculptures like these, di Suvero makes the point that constructions of steel beams are unlimited in their expressive potential.

Balance is a basic issue for yet another successor to David Smith, Richard Serra, who explores it in ways that generate kinesthetic responses and perceptual investigations. In his *Inverted House of Cards* (1969–70, p. 261), the four identical roughly five-foot-tall slabs of steel stand erect and meet in such a way as to create a small column of space in the center. Since these upright slabs stand on their own, unfooted and without supports, their balance suggests imbalance. This tension creates a consciousness of stability and instability as human constants, and a sense of how much an assumption of balance shapes the way we see the world. Serra's *My Curves Are Not Mad* (1987, pp. 262–63) consists of two parallel nearly forty-five-foot-long arcs of steel that lean into each other, creating a contracting and expanding passageway between them. The tilt of the arcs, with all their massive weight, is experienced physically, so that the viewer's body feels tilted and unbalanced in their presence. This imbalance creates a heightened awareness of the weight of the present, the weight of the body, the weight of gravity, and the drama of the most elementary acts, like standing, walking, and looking. For Serra, the experience of imbalance is essential to awareness.

Although in his hands-off, modular approach and in his black, uninflected surfaces, Tony

Smith seems almost diametrically opposed to David Smith, this architect-sculptor-painter also had strong ties with Abstract Expressionism and a profound interest in the unconscious and myth, and he, too, found in imbalance enormous potential for psychological and philosophical meaning. The ten irregular parts in his *Ten Elements* (1975–79, fabricated 1980, pp. 246–47) are related, yet different, like members of a family. Each part has something odd about the way it sits on the ground. Each faces out, with a facet of its shell as eager for the sun as a cat on a windowsill; yet each also turns inward. Like so many of the other sculptures that explore balance, each of the forms has something circuslike about it, as if it is working out and getting ready to perform. The imbalance underlines Smith's belief that each reality has different sides. What is just as essential, and just as modern, about the ten forms is their unpredictability. How they appear from one side cannot always be predicted from another, and which side reveals itself depends not only on the observer's viewpoint but also upon where the form is placed, which forms are around it, and the time of day. In *Ten Elements*, imbalance creates an awareness of the complexity of personality. It can also inspire a meditation on what it means to know.

One of the sculptor-poets of imbalance who has more affinity with Tony Smith than with David Smith is Martin Puryear, whose *Night and Day* (1984, pp. 304–05) suggests quite different ways in which the idea of imbalance can be developed. The sculpture is a wooden semicircle—perhaps like one line of a rainbow—nearly ten feet wide and seven feet tall, suspended against the wall. The left half of the arc is painted white, the right half black. The sculpture suggests a fusion, but the sides are not equal. The white side touches the floor; the black side dangles. At the foot of the white side, between its curved line and the floor, is a lean wedge-shaped form that is square on the bottom. At the end of the dark side is a squat, black rocklike form. The white wedge shape seems self-absorbed, blissfully what it is. The black shape has irregular facets, like a crystal, which make it seem as if it is looking around. While unanchored, unable to find solid ground, it has consciousness and movement. The imbalance suggests a witty and affectionate but pointed metaphor, perhaps about a personal relationship. It also suggests a statement about race relations in America.

Perhaps *the* sculptor-poet of imbalance is Joel Shapiro, whose work is as hard to imagine without David Smith as is the work of Caro, di Suvero, and Serra. In his *Untitled* (1983, p. 277), one short and one longer line are attached at right angles, at what is the abstracted figure's waist, and then leaned back so that the tilt suggests both the back of Rodin's *Monument to Balzac* and the legs and back of Duchamp-Villon's *Large Horse* (1914; enlargement, fabricated 1966; p. 129). The way it is folded at the waist is an indication of Shapiro's respect for Matisse's sculptures, such as *Large Seated Nude*.[7] With Shapiro, however, the formal exploration is no more important than the human statement that is made available by the investigation of form. The figure could be bowing or pulling back or getting ready to coil like a snake. For Shapiro, the study of balance becomes a way of bringing together and intensifying different and often violently conflicting emotions, and, like Serra, encouraging viewers to experience anew basic feelings and actions.

In *Untitled* (1985–87, p. 279), Shapiro made the impossible seem possible. The legs are in the position of a split. The weight is supported on one arm while the other rises nearly straight into the air. The figure, struggling to hold itself up, appears to be collapsing. But it is also moving its arms or stretching, like a dancer. And in the way the raised arm reaches for the sky, it is theatrically heroic. Like Matisse, Shapiro proceeded from a profound perception of the body's center of gravity in the hip and stomach area, which he set slightly above the ground, giving the body and its movements a necessary sense of elasticity. Shapiro's treatment of the body's center of gravity and the way muscles and limbs are joined makes it possible for viewers to experience kinesthetically the sculptural movements. In Shapiro's work, the body, like the mind, can be continually rediscovered and reinvented. Through an exploration of imbalance, Shapiro makes contradiction, convulsiveness, grandeur, pathos, delight, and play part of our physical nature.

Pressure

A distinguishing characteristic of some of the most enduring sculpture is the experience of pressure it creates. Usually, the pressure emanates from within the mass. In Egyptian sculpture, for example, it may come from the weight and compression of the carved stone, which can make a seated pharaoh seem such a concentration of physical and spiritual power that his authority is impregnable. In Aztec sculpture, the pressure communicates titanic energy coiled within the stone, which can make a snake god seem so forbidding that the human body seems hopelessly frail and even irrelevant in comparison. In many of the splendid hu, jiu, and dou vessels from Bronze Age China, the bellies are so firmly shaped and elegantly swollen that these objects of everyday life could have made their powerful owners appear to be holding a sacred breath.

From the Renaissance until Modernism, Western sculpture rarely exerted comparable authority. There are exceptions, of which the most notable examples are by Michelangelo and Bernini, two artist-architects whose pictorial and architectural intelligence contributed to their astonishing spatial imaginations. In settings Michelangelo designed, his sculptures are pressure points that activate an intense awareness of the power and purpose of stone and space. His freestanding sculptures acknowledge space but they tend to pull it into themselves so they become magnets of light and energy. Bernini, with his feeling for surface and light and his theatrical flair, could make a figure or narrative in a church so emotionally active, expressively concentrated, and architecturally integral that not only this figure or narrative but also sculpture itself seemed indispensable to his culture's secular and spiritual existence.

When sculpture creates such experiences of physical and spatial pressure, it becomes irrefutable and fulfills a basic human need to feel spirit and thought embodied in matter. It does so by arguing that sculpture can indeed be touched by and convey something beyond matter—that sculptors can gain access to some shape or form of spiritual energy or presence when it is this energy or presence that they are determined to encounter. Above all, the experience of pressure lets viewers know that the sculpture generating it is defined by an intensity of perception, a quality of concentration, and a force of belief that, together, are always a sign of a first-rate sculptural imagination.

Among Modernist sculptors, many of whom were inspired by pre-Renaissance and non-Western art—including Egyptian (which influenced Duchamp-Villon, Paul Gauguin, Giacometti, and Picasso) and pre-Columbian painting and sculpture (which influenced Henry Moore)[8]—pressure became, once again, an essential sculptural characteristic. However, the meanings associated with pressure and the ways of creating it are far more varied, and the interests it serves are markedly different from those in the past. The basic challenge was this: before Modernism, sculptural pressure served power. In ancient Egypt and China and in Aztec Mexico, sculptural compression reflected rigidly hierarchical societies that were closed, if not sealed. How could the experience of pressure be created in skeptical, mobile societies that have seemed to change by the minute and in which institutional power has provoked as much suspicion as respect?

In Modernist sculpture, generating an experience of pressure becomes as much a way of questioning authority as it is of affirming and celebrating it. In sculptures by Abakanowicz, Brancusi, Duchamp-Villon, Giacometti, Antony Gormley, Picasso, Matisse, Rodin, Rosso, Serra, and so many others, something fateful and definitive has happened, but the situations, or dramas, are at the same time inconclusive and open-ended. Modernist sculptures build a sense of inevitability yet work against it. In Rodin's *The Age of Bronze*, for example, it is not the force of what has been already done to the young man but the surge of his inner life—of that which is not yet fully formed—that creates the strongest experience of pressure in the work. In Serra's *My Curves Are Not Mad*, the steel arcs, so massive that they seem immovable, confront anyone in their presence with an experience of tremendous physical authority. But the pressure that establishes the authority of Serra's sculpture is not intended to serve institutional power. In fact it is meant to enable viewers to feel in their bodies the realities of gravity, balance, and movement, and then to encourage consciousness of how these realities are shaped or manipulated by environmental conditions. In Modernist sculpture, pressure tends to place viewers in existential situations in which they have to figure out what to think and where to go next.

The issue that connects many ways of creating pressure, and that does the most to illuminate the importance of the experience of pressure to Modernist sculptural aesthetics—and what may link it to the experience of pressure in older sculpture—is survival. No other century has seen as much death as this one and lived with such a keen awareness that the human race could destroy itself overnight. No other century has felt more acutely the realities and consequences of political, religious, racial, ethnic, and sexual violence.

Concern with survival, and with finding an alternative to institutional authority, drives the organic tradition that began with Rodin and Brancusi. In Arp's *Torso with Buds* (1961, p. 235), with its blooming and flirtatious plant-body, and Moore's *Three Piece No. 3: Vertebrae* (1968, pp. 252–53), with its Rosso-like depiction of a garden conversation among gregarious bones, the surging energy within the mass suggests the presence of a life force that will endure. Here and wherever else the pressure of this organic vitality can be felt—in works ranging from Henri Laurens's *Grande Maternité* (1932, cast 1965, p. 173) and Picasso's *Pregnant Woman (second state)* (1950/59, p. 115) to many contemporary sculptures by Abakanowicz and Puryear—the flow and swell of the mass are tactile. The artists have not only brought into sculpture the presence of an inexorable yet forever moldable will to live, a will that cannot be killed, but they have done so in ways that encourage viewers to feel they can somehow put their hands on it, take hold of it, and make it their own.

Concern with survival also drives perhaps the most distinct and powerful expression of modern sculptural pressure: the tension between figure and space. This tension already existed in embryonic form in Rodin's *The Age of Bronze*, where the interior and exterior of the figure suggest separate realities, and light embraces, even grips, the figure's solid mass as new life begins to push out within it. In Picasso's *Head (Fernande)* (1909, p. 111), a head-landscape is broken into facets so that space flows in and over them, exploring them with such freedom that the authority of the mass is no longer inviolable. Space and mass had become separate realities, and although they are not pitted against each other in Picasso's landmark work, it is clear that from Cubism on, space could engage mass in a way that is so hungry, competitive, or intrusive that mass has all it can do to hold its own.

Survival and space were decisive issues in Giacometti's work from the time he joined the Surrealists in 1930. In *No More Play* (1931–32, p. 149), two tiny standing figures are stranded in the desolate fields of a landscape that is meant to be—as the work's title implies—some kind of game board. Separating the figurines, in the middle of the board, is what looks like a graveyard. Space here, no matter how dominant, is not invasive. It does not lean against the figures but flows around them, overwhelming them in scale and making them seem insignificant. The power of space comes from its vastness, not from voracious or destructive intent.

Between 1942 and 1945, Giacometti was holed up in Geneva, with warring nations surrounding neutral Switzerland on all sides. In a tiny hotel room, he began to model his plaster figures down to the size of the figurines in *No More Play*, and sometimes, with one or two last gestures, they completely disintegrated. In modeling sculptures no more than a few inches tall, like those in *Two Figurines* (ca. 1945, p. 153), Giacometti's experience of space changed. Space no longer appears to freely circulate around the figures but presses against them. The pull of space and light into the passive but expectant bodies exerts pressure so intense that the figures seem near some final point of existence. For Giacometti, space had become pressure, and it took on a new kind of sculptural identity. It had become so dense and physical that it is itself sculptural in feeling.[9]

After World War II, space became a crucible through which Giacometti's figures must pass. It is as if the pressure space exerts upon them has engulfed them in a new human condition defined by precariousness and threat. And it is only by wading through space, or standing as immobilized as Ulysses roped to a mast and enduring it, that the full destructive and creative potential of this condition can be understood. In *Venice Woman III* (1956, p. 163), space leans into the standing figure, squeezing her—even, it seems, modeling her, and at times coming close to swallowing her up. Her eyes stare outward, frozen, even horrified, but as she withstands her trial, she also may be looking across a threshold onto something she is normally forbidden to see but that the pressure of space now permits her to see. Within Giacometti's sculptural space, the pressures of danger and death make possible an experience of a realm beyond the worlds of flesh and language. Having the courage to live the threat in a raw, even pure state, brings with it the possibility for transgressive awareness and revelation.

A less noted but perhaps equally decisive shift in the nature of sculptural space took place in the work of David Smith. Inspired by the steel sculptures of Picasso and González and the Surrealist sculptures of Giacometti, Smith rejected the monolith from the time he began welding steel in the early 1930s. After World War II, his steel lines stop imposing themselves on space. Rather, they release space to be itself and in the process enable themselves to be touched by its powers of enchantment and freedom. In *The Forest* (1950, p. 181), Smith turned industrially made sawtoothed implements into tree presences with birdlike forms clinging to their branches. In the plane in front of the trees is a ledge, shaped like an anvil—a piece of hardware that was one of Smith's instruments of creation—on top of which are perched four forms, one of them suggesting Brancusi's birds. The enchantment of the work comes partly from the startling inventiveness and placement of the imagery and partly from the no-less-startling transformation of undistinguished industrial objects into fairy-tale creatures of nature. It also comes from the spell cast by space, which seems so pleased to circulate freely in and around the forms that it consecrates the sculpture simply by making itself totally at home.

By the time he made *Voltri VI* (1962, p. 189), Smith's sculptural space had become much more physical; space had become pressure. The sculpture consists of two roughly eight-foot-tall steel silhouettes, slightly separated, placed back to back, on a construction resembling an unhitched wagon. Smith described the work as "a tong with wheels and two end clouds. One cloud rests in the spoon—each cloud end goes up from the tongue unsupported."[10] Space presses into the irregular concavities of the "clouds." More important, space appears to solidify for a moment in the thin vertical strip between the two silhouettes. This vertical opening, with the shape of a Barnett Newman–like line, becomes as sculptural in feeling as the steel. In this and a number of other sculptures Smith made after 1950, space is as sculptural as any in twentieth-century art. Because of its pressure, it is a space that is experienced in terms of authority, but it is not dangerous—as long as it is unimpeded. On the contrary, for Smith, who had a permanent residence in the Adirondack Mountains from 1940 until his death in 1965, space came to represent nature and spirit and the kind of absolute freedom he was reaching for in his art. In his last years, space did not test his allusive and totemic constructions so much as explore and embrace them. The pressure of space became an assurance that Smith had made contact with something godly. It became not a threat to survival but an assurance of survival. Smith brought into American sculpture an experience of space similar to the one that shaped Abstract Expressionist painting. Many of the approaches to American sculpture in nature that proliferated in the 1960s and 1970s, including earthworks, grew out of a kind of sculptural pressure that may be unprecedented in the history of art.

Enchantment

Given that everything about the language of sculpture had to be thought about freshly, that everything about form could, as a result, be loaded with intention, and that sculptors with the will and talent to rethink sculptural language and form were preoccupied with issues of the body, nature, and survival, it is not surprising that Modernist sculpture has been essential to the experience and formation of culture. Modernist sculpture encourages discovery and thought. It is an act of healing. It continues to inspire many people to believe that any kind of human experience, no matter how desperate, can, through the processes and materials of sculpture, become a source of understanding and transformation. With Modernism, making sculpture became what it had been much earlier and still is in many cultures outside the West, a magical act.

The widespread conviction among Modernist sculptors that in order to be alive and effective sculpture had to be enchanted can be suggested by the allure of animals and a belief in their connection to wonder and ritual. In the Nasher Collection, Alexander Calder's *The Spider* (1940, p. 193), Max Ernst's goat-fish in *Capricorn* (1948, cast 1963–64, p. 205), Barry Flanagan's *Large Leaping Hare* (1982, p. 293), Joan Miró's *Moonbird* (1944–46; enlargement, 1966, cast 1967; p. 211), David Smith's birds in *The Forest*, and Tony Smith's *The Snake Is Out* (1962, fabricated 1981, pp. 242–43) were all made with great affection. All have the kind of popular appeal that suggests the need among many Modernist sculptors to captivate not only adults but also children. The prevalence of animals that are meant to cast spells as they do in fables is an unmistakable sign that as a group Modernist sculptors, including Abakanowicz, Brancusi, Giacometti, Picasso, and Puryear, have respected the deep need in many people— especially all those in this century who have witnessed or lived through displacement and rupture—to be delighted and enthralled.

One principle of Modernist enchantment is its resistance to absolute distinctions between cultures, places, and times. Modernist sculpture has brought together categories, feelings, and realms assumed to be irreconcilable. No psychological or social split is considered inherently unbridgeable. In principle, anything can be wedded to anything else, and in the surprise and inventiveness of the synthesis, a spell can be cast, differences reconciled, a wound healed. One reason Picasso's *Head (Fernande)* is so fascinating is that it not only produces a collision between space and mass but also merges an urbane French woman, Fernande Olivier, with the almost medieval Spanish landscape of Horta de Ebro, where Picasso spent the crucial summer of 1909. The reason John Storrs's *Study in Architectural Forms (Forms in Space)* (1927, p. 167) has such charm is that an image of impersonal skyscrapers also suggests such divergent readings as oars and a nuclear family.

What is the possibility of enchantment when compatibility is not possible? When considering the relationship between human beings and machines—which has been a recurrent theme in twentieth-century sculpture, running through the work of John Chamberlain, David Smith, Storrs, and others in the Nasher Collection—some sculptors have found primarily conflict. In *Large Horse*, Duchamp-Villon expressed the relationship between human being and machine, and between rural and urban, ancient and modern, as both a union and a collision. In this hybrid image—which was already at an advanced stage when World War I began in August 1914 but which Duchamp-Villon continued to work on after he enlisted as a medical officer—the sculptor declared his belief in the power of machines and their development from nature, but he also declared just as strongly his apprehension about technological power and its potential to destroy human beings' intimate connections with themselves and nature. Because of its ambivalence, the work has an enduring edge. It is hard, however, for a warning to be enchanted. When there is doubt about transformation and healing, as there is here, there may be compelling and necessary art, but there is little or no enchantment.

In sculptures by the Russian Constructivists, on the other hand, the relationship between the natural and technological could be a harmonious and indeed enchanted marriage. Gabo's *Linear Construction in Space No. 1 (Variation)* (1942–43; enlargement, ca. 1957–58; p. 199) is a hymn to hope composed at another very dark time. The way the sculpture is strung suggests the lyricism of stringed instruments and mathematics, as well as the lightness and resiliency of industrial materials like nylon and plastic. The sculpture is also extremely organic, even sexual, in the way the ellipse in the center seems to fold open like petals, allowing space to pass through. The organic is thoroughly compatible with the mathematical and industrial; it exists inside them, almost as if it were their womb. This harmony of organic, musical, and technological creates the sense of a modern magic.[11]

Another essential principle of Modernist sculpture, and of Modernist enchantment, is unpredictability. One of the most effective ways of establishing the impact of this principle has been through appropriating and assembling found objects, often encountered by chance. Integrating them into a new artistic reality, the meanings hidden or dormant within their familiar contexts could emerge. When they did emerge, they could demonstrate that everyday life was itself a source of magic. In Picasso's *Pregnant Woman*, parts of three water pitchers are incorporated into belly and breasts so miraculously fluid and sensual that they are irresistible to the eye and hand. Miró assembled a great many sculptures from found objects, including *Caress of a Bird* (1967, p. 213), in which a straw hat or basket (the head) and a tortoise shell (the abdomen or genitals) take their places in a starry-eyed and sexually available female presence who appears, because of the objects with which she was assembled, to be invested with the power of a prophet or priest.

One of the most important manifestations of the power of unpredictability is suddenness. Suddenness can suggest newness, freshness, and immanence, as it does in the decisively influential paintings of Picasso, so many of which, no matter how prodigiously complex, look as if they had spontaneously emerged. Suddenness can also suggest the mystery of being—the mystery that anything exists at all—as well as the way anyone or anything can surface and vanish in an instant. The prevalence of images of suddenness reflects both an insistence on the moment and a profound awareness of transience and loss. Whatever ideas and feelings may be attached to it, suddenness communicates a will to be, an assertion of existence, a determination to survive, that cannot be denied.

Suddenness is a characteristic of Brancusi's sculpture and of sculpture by artists who are in some way his offspring. *Nancy Cunard* is an example of a Brancusi that grows and turns in several directions but somehow still seems the expression of an iconic instant. Ellsworth Kelly's approximately ten-foot-tall bronze stele, *Untitled* (1986, p. 313), was conceived through a Brancusi-like attention to line, surface, and shape, but it is symmetrical, unlike Brancusi's work, and, more than the Brancusi, it stands in place so integrally that attention is constantly drawn to the sculpture as a whole. A no-less-powerful experience of suddenness is offered by Duchamp-Villon's *Maggy* (1912, cast 1957, p. 123), which reflects Brancusi's preference for clean, well-lighted shapes, but it, like the Kelly, is symmetrical, and its pronounced bulbous features, sprouting from the exceptionally long and tubular neck, create the sense of a mesmerizing, larger-than-life authority who is part guardian-concierge, part witch.

The experience of suddenness is no less essential to two sculptors who were influenced by Brancusi in less obvious ways. The thirty-six figures in Abakanowicz's *Bronze Crowd* seem to have shot up, to have gathered all at once, on command, and to be waiting for another command at which point they will, all at once, march together or disperse.[12] In David Smith's *The Forest*, there is a similar sense of a sculpture that has just happened and that will retain its responsiveness to the moment as long as it exists. With Smith, as with Abakanowicz, this immediacy depended not only upon formal mastery but also upon a formidable creative energy and will that, in his case, particularly after World War II, was always emphatically turned outward, toward the world.

One of Modernism's great contributions to the enchantment of sculpture was its rethinking of scale. No one now has to be told about the enlargement of sculpture after World War II: it got bigger and bigger and bigger until it could become a jetty or a field. Claes Oldenburg—long before Jeff Koons, another sculptor represented in the Nasher Collection—explored, almost systematically, the possibilities of taking a common object and making a sculpture of it in another material, in a different context, and on a radically larger scale. His *Typewriter Eraser* (1976, p. 233) is a more-than-seven-foot-tall monument in cement, stainless steel, and aluminum of what was, before word processors, an insignificant but indispensable item of office life. The changes in material and scale make the sculpture look as animated and fanciful as the stuff of fable.

The Nasher Collection also makes it possible to consider the power of sculpture that is so dramatically reduced in size that it almost seems to have shrunk. A number of sculptors in the collection, notably Gormley and Shapiro, have made tiny as well as monumental sculptures, and the tiny sculptures are essential to the physical and psychological pressures their bodies of work exert. Such sculpture has been important to the exploration of anxiety and crisis. It has also been important to the accessibility and democratization of art. Sculpture that can be grasped by the hand is highly personal. When successful, it is talismanic.

A little more than three inches tall, *Portrait of Professor Gosset* (1918, cast 1960s, p. 131) is, aside from Giacometti's *Two Figurines*, the smallest sculpture in the collection. Duchamp-Villon made it when he was in the hospital struggling to recuperate from the typhoid fever he had contracted in 1916; Gosset was his doctor. It was Duchamp-Villon's last sculpture, worked on shortly before he died at the age of forty-two. The swell of the forehead, nose, and chin is emphasized; the cavities of the eyes and mouth are sunk in shadow. The image is simultaneously streamlined and ancient; modern and primitive power have merged. Just as important, the head was modeled so as to allow the owner's hand to know it. Fingers can cling to its features in the night. As powerfully visual as it is, it is as much a sculpture for the blind as Brancusi's nearly seven-inch-tall, twelve-inch-long marble *Sculpture for the Blind (I)* (1920?, Philadelphia Museum of Art): it can be experienced by touch alone. It is a response to extreme danger and frailty, and it is an expression of imagination and prayer.[13] Its magic is in the inventiveness with sculptural language, but it is also in the intention that drives it and in the spirit within the form. In its responsiveness to the urgency of the present, to the mysteries of space and night, and to the knowledge of the past, it is an utterance of a kind only sculpture can emit.

Notes

1. In this essay, I use the word "Modernist" to refer not only to clearly identifiable Modernists but also to contemporary sculptors whose work sustains Modernist traditions. The full relationship to Modernist traditions of contemporary sculptors collected by Patsy and Raymond Nasher can only be appropriately addressed in an independent study.

2. In her insightful discussion of Rodin, Rosalind E. Krauss referred to the "way he related, or failed to relate, the outward appearance of the body to its inner structure"; see Krauss, *Passages in Modern Sculpture* (Cambridge, Mass.: M.I.T. Press, 1981), p. 23. Two sculptors with work in the Nasher Collection, have made eloquent remarks about *The Age of Bronze*; see William Tucker's influential *The Language of Sculpture* (London: Thames and Hudson, 1974), chapter 1, and "Antony Gormley: Interview with Declan McGonagle," in *Antony Gormley*, exh. cat. (London: Tate Gallery Publications, 1993), p. 50. Alain Kirili, the contemporary sculptor who has written the most about Rodin, is also represented in the Nasher Collection; see Kirili, *Statuaire* (Paris: Denoël, 1986), and Kirili and Philippe Sollers, *Rodin: Dessins Érotiques* (Paris: Gallimard, 1987). Kirili has also written passionately about other artists in the Nasher Collection, including Giacometti, Barnett Newman, and David Smith. His sculptural dialogues with Modernism are so particular and so sustained that, in order to do justice to them, his sculptures almost need to be explored in a context they set for themselves. For an overview of *The Age of Bronze*, including a discussion of the changing of its title from *The Vanquished*, see Ruth Butler, *Rodin: The Shape of Genius* (New Haven: Yale University Press, 1993), chapter 9.

3. In the series of sculptures, called *Newborn*, he developed between 1915 and 1932, Brancusi made the cry of a child into a condition. I have wondered if the purity, seamlessness, and historylessness of Brancusi's abstractions did not have something to do with a need to smooth over and repair the wounds he had suffered as a child.

4. For more on Abakanowicz's use of the crowd, see Michael Brenson, "The Abakanowicz Crowd," in *Where Is Abel, Thy Brother?*, exh. cat. (Warsaw: Zacheta Gallery of Contemporary Art, 1995), unpaginated. For more on Abakanowicz's relationships to Brancusi and Rodin, see Brenson, "Magdalena Abakanowicz and Modern Sculpture," in *Magdalena Abakanowicz: Recent Sculpture*, exh. cat. (Providence: Museum of Art, Rhode Island School of Design, 1993), pp. 9–21. For more on Abakanowicz and sculptural interiority, see Brenson, *Magdalena Abakanowicz's "War Games": Monumental Horizontality*, exh. cat. (New York: Institute for Contemporary Art, P.S. 1 Museum, 1993).

5. The relationship of the diagonal to the curve at the foot of *Monument to Balzac* is very close to the relationship of the diagonal to the swell at the foot of Brancusi's many versions of *Bird in Space* made over more than twenty years. It is also worth mentioning how much the slightly open mouth and emerging utterance in *The Age of Bronze* predicts the open mouths and far greater sense of release in many of Brancusi's sculptures of birds.

6. David Smith quoted in Cleve Gray, ed., *David Smith by David Smith: Sculpture and Writings* (London: Thames and Hudson, 1968), p. 68.

7. Shapiro referred to Matisse's sculpture in Peter Boswell's "An Interview with Joel Shapiro," in *Joel Shapiro Outdoors*, exh. cat. (Minneapolis: Walker Art Center; Kansas City, Mo.: Nelson-Atkins Museum of Art, 1995), pp. 33–37.

8. The Nashers assembled an exceptional collection of pre-Columbian sculpture, as well as a major collection of Guatemalan textiles that was donated to the Dallas Museum of Art in 1986.

9. David Sylvester offered new observations about Giacometti's tiny figures in his *Looking at Giacometti* (New York: Henry Holt, 1994), chapter 9. The most comprehensive discussion of the context in which Giacometti made these figures is in James Lord, *Giacometti: A Biography* (New York: Farrar, Straus and Giroux, 1985), chapters 32–37.

10. David Smith quoted in *A Century of Modern Sculpture: The Patsy and Raymond Nasher Collection*, exh. cat. (New York: Rizzoli, 1987), p. 195.

11. For a full description of this work and also a discussion of Gabo's *Linear Construction in Space No. 2* (1945/58, Solomon R. Guggenheim Museum), see Steven A. Nash, "Naum Gabo: Sculptures of Purity and Possibility," in Nash and Jorn Merkert, eds., *Naum Gabo: Sixty Years of Constructivism* (Munich: Prestel-Verlag, 1985), pp. 37–41.

12. Abakanowicz has spoken about the "bewitching power" art must have and about the magic in objects from New Guinea. See Michael Brenson, "Survivor Art," *New York Times Magazine*, Nov. 29, 1992, pp. 50, 52.

13. In her discussion of a related head, Judith Zilczer suggested that the *Portrait of Professor Gosset* may also combine an image of gas masks, symbols of the new kind of technological horror he experienced firsthand in World War I, with the healing magic of African masks. See Zilczer, "In the Face of War: The Last Works of Raymond Duchamp-Villon," *Art Bulletin*, March 1983, pp. 138–44.

CATALOGUE

AUGUSTE RODIN

The Age of Bronze (L'Age d'airain), ca. 1876

Plaster

71 1/2 x 21 1/4 x 25 1/2 inches (181.6 x 54 x 64.8 cm)

AUGUSTE RODIN

Eve, 1881

Bronze
68 x 17 1/4 x 25 1/2 inches (172.7 x 43.8 x 64.8 cm)
Cast before 1932

AUGUSTE RODIN

Study for the Monument to Balzac (Balzac, dernière étude), ca. 1897

Bronze

44 1/4 x 17 1/4 x 15 inches (112.4 x 43.8 x 38.1 cm)

Marked 6, cast 1974

AUGUSTE RODIN

Head of Balzac (Balzac, tête), 1897

Plaster

7 ½ x 8 x 6 ½ inches (19 x 20.3 x 16.5 cm)

AUGUSTE RODIN

Hanako, 1908

Plaster

6 3/4 x 4 5/8 x 5 1/2 inches (17.1 x 11.7 x 14 cm)

MEDARDO ROSSO

The Concierge (La Portinaia), ca. 1883–84

Wax over plaster

15 x 13 3/8 x 7 1/16 inches (38.1 x 34 x 17.9 cm)

MEDARDO ROSSO

The Golden Age (L'Eta d'oro, also called **Aetas aurea**), 1886

Wax over plaster

19 x 18 1/4 x 14 inches (48.3 x 46.4 x 35.6 cm)

MEDARDO ROSSO

Sick Child (Bambino malato), 1889

Wax over plaster

10 5/8 x 10 x 7 1/4 inches (27 x 25.4 x 18.4 cm)

MEDARDO ROSSO

Jewish Child (**Bambino ebreo**), ca. 1892–93

Wax over plaster

8 5/8 x 7 x 5 7/8 inches (21.9 x 17.8 x 14.9 cm)

Cast 1900–14

PAUL GAUGUIN

Torso of a Woman (Torse d'une femme), ca. 1896

Low-fired clay

11 1/2 x 5 1/4 x 6 1/2 inches (29.2 x 13.3 x 16.5 cm)

PAUL GAUGUIN

Tahitian Girl, ca. 1896

Wood and mixed media

37 3/8 x 7 1/2 x 8 inches (94.9 x 19 x 20.3 cm)

HENRI MATISSE

Madeleine I, 1901

Painted plaster

23 3/4 x 9 1/2 x 7 1/2 inches (60.3 x 24.1 x 19 cm)

Cast 1903

HENRI MATISSE

Standing Nude, Arms on Head (Nu debout, les bras lévés), 1906

Bronze

10 1/4 x 5 1/4 x 4 1/4 inches (26 x 13.3 x 10.8 cm)

Marked 3/10

HENRI MATISSE

Reclining Nude (I) Aurora (Nu couché [I] Aurore), 1906–07

Bronze

13 1/16 x 19 3/4 x 11 inches (33.2 x 50.2 x 27.9 cm)

Marked 3/10

HENRI MATISSE

Head with Necklace (La Femme au collier), 1907

Bronze

5 7/8 x 5 1/8 x 3 3/4 inches (14.9 x 13 x 9.5 cm)

Marked 9/10

HENRI MATISSE

Two Women (Groupe de femmes, also called

Deux Négresses [Groupe de deux jeunes filles]), 1907

Bronze

18 3/8 x 10 1/2 x 7 1/2 inches (46.7 x 26.7 x 19 cm)

Marked 8/10

HENRI MATISSE

Decorative Figure (Figure décorative), 1908

Bronze

28 3/8 x 20 3/8 x 12 3/8 inches (72.1 x 51.8 x 31.4 cm)

Marked 2/10, cast early 1930s

HENRI MATISSE

Large Seated Nude (Grand Nu assis), ca. 1925–29

Bronze

30 1/2 x 31 5/8 x 13 5/8 inches (77.5 x 80.3 x 34.6 cm)

Marked 9/10

HENRI MATISSE

Tiari (Le Tiaré), 1930 (two views)

Bronze

9 5/8 x 7 7/8 x 5 5/8 inches (24.4 x 20 x 14.3 cm)

Marked 3/10

(pages 96–97)

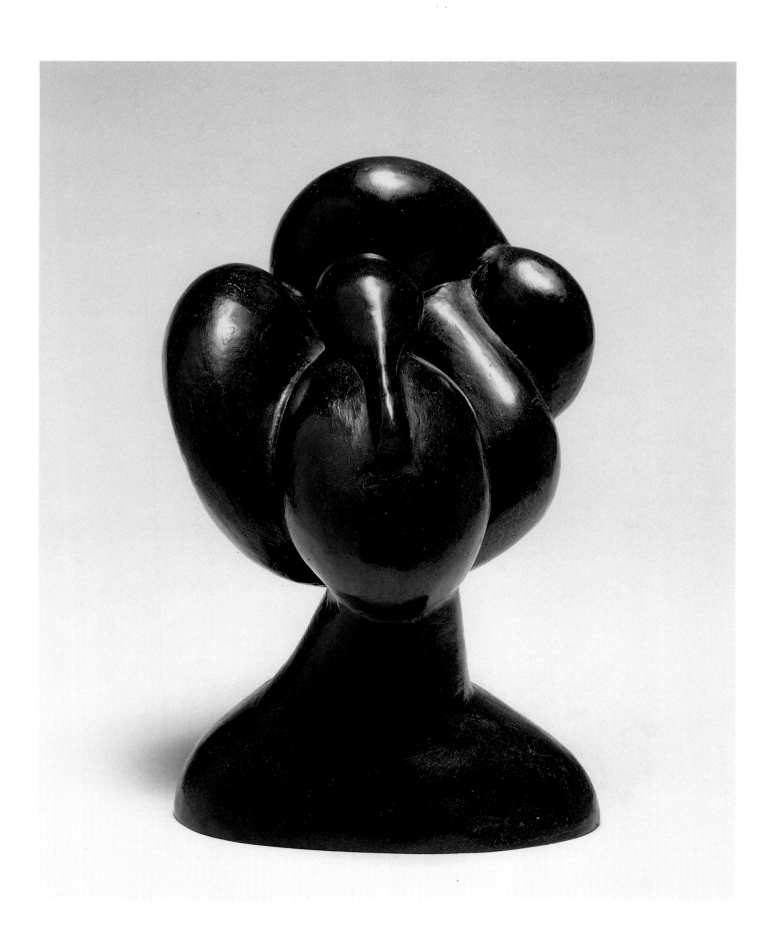

HENRI MATISSE

Venus in a Shell (second state) (Vénus à la coquille [2ème état]), 1932·

Bronze
13 ³/₈ x 6 ⁷/₈ x 9 ¹/₈ inches (34 x 17.5 x 23.2 cm)
Marked 4/10

ARISTIDE MAILLOL

Night (La Nuit), ca. 1902–09

Bronze

41 x 42 x 22 ¹/₂ inches (104.1 x 106.7 x 57.2 cm)

Marked E.A. (artist's proof), cast 1960

ARISTIDE MAILLOL

Marie, ca. 1930

Bronze

27 x 8 x 13 inches (68.6 x 20.3 x 33 cm)

Marked 5/6

CONSTANTIN BRANCUSI

Bust of a Boy (Buste d'enfant), 1906

Bronze

12 1/4 x 8 x 7 inches (31.1 x 20.3 x 17.8 cm)

CONSTANTIN BRANCUSI

The Kiss (Le Baiser), 1907–08

Plaster

11 x 10 1/4 x 8 1/2 inches (27.9 x 26 x 21.6 cm)

Cast before 1914

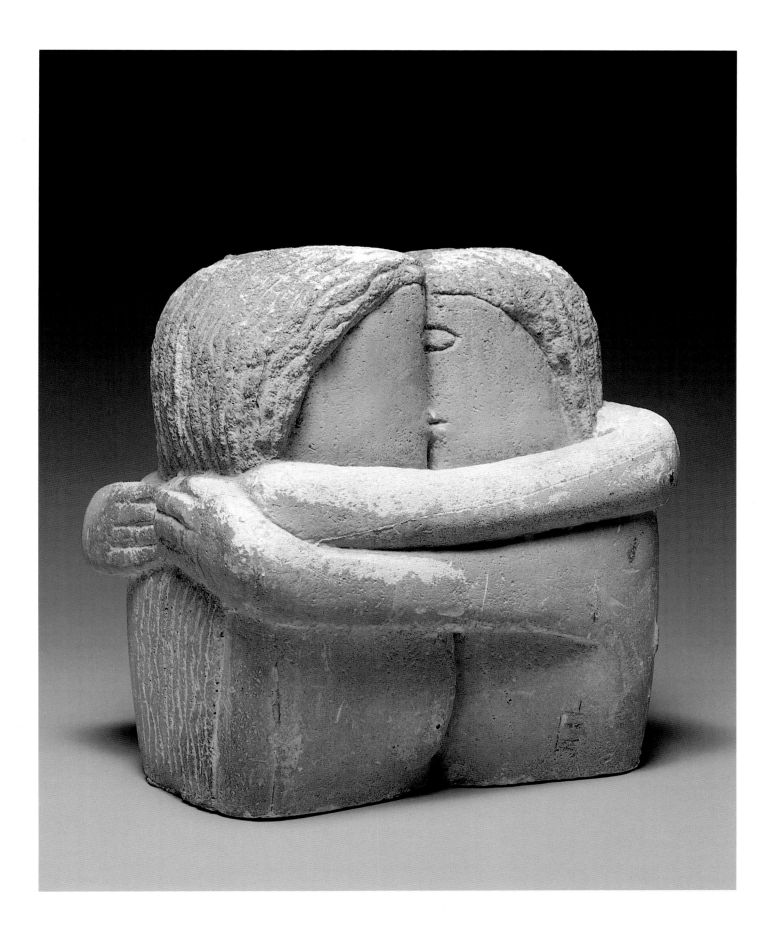

CONSTANTIN BRANCUSI

Nancy Cunard (Sophisticated Young Lady)

(Nancy Cunard [Jeune fille sophistiquée]), 1925–27

Walnut, on marble base

24 3/4 x 12 1/2 x 4 3/8 inches (62.9 x 31.8 x 11.1 cm)

The Patsy and Raymond Nasher Collection at The Nelson-Atkins Museum of Art,

Kansas City, Missouri, Lent by the Hall Family Foundation

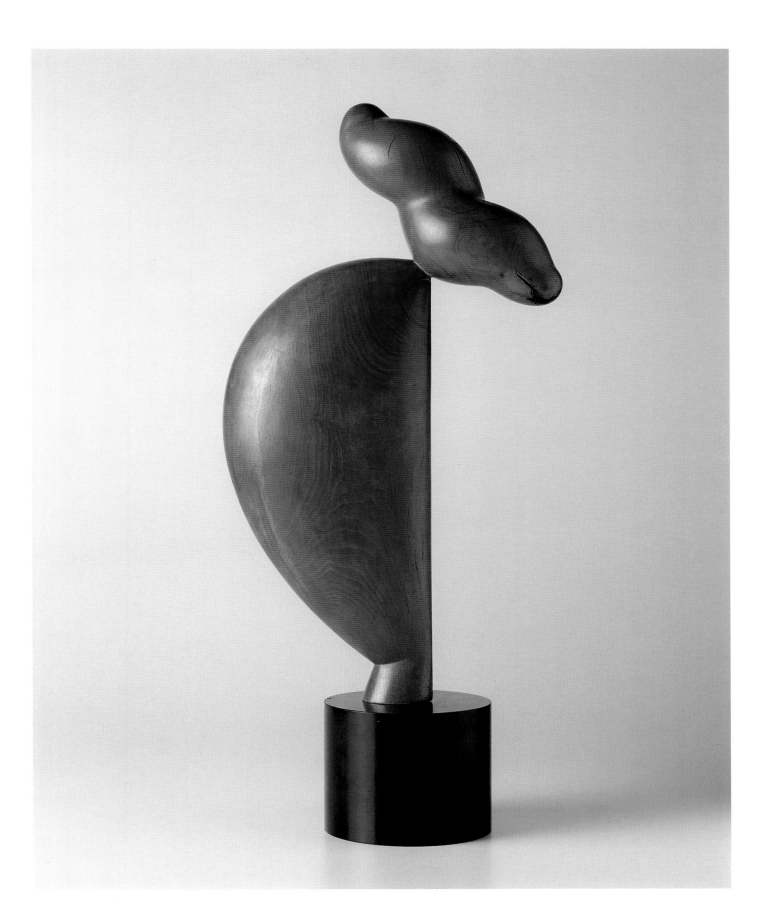

PABLO PICASSO

Head (Fernande) (Tête de femme [Fernande]), 1909

Plaster

18 1/2 x 14 1/8 x 13 3/4 inches (47 x 35.9 x 34.9 cm)

PABLO PICASSO

Head of a Woman (Tête de femme), 1931 (two views)

Bronze

34 x 14 3/8 x 19 1/4 inches (86.4 x 36.5 x 48.9 cm)

Marked 1/2, cast 1973

(pages 112–13)

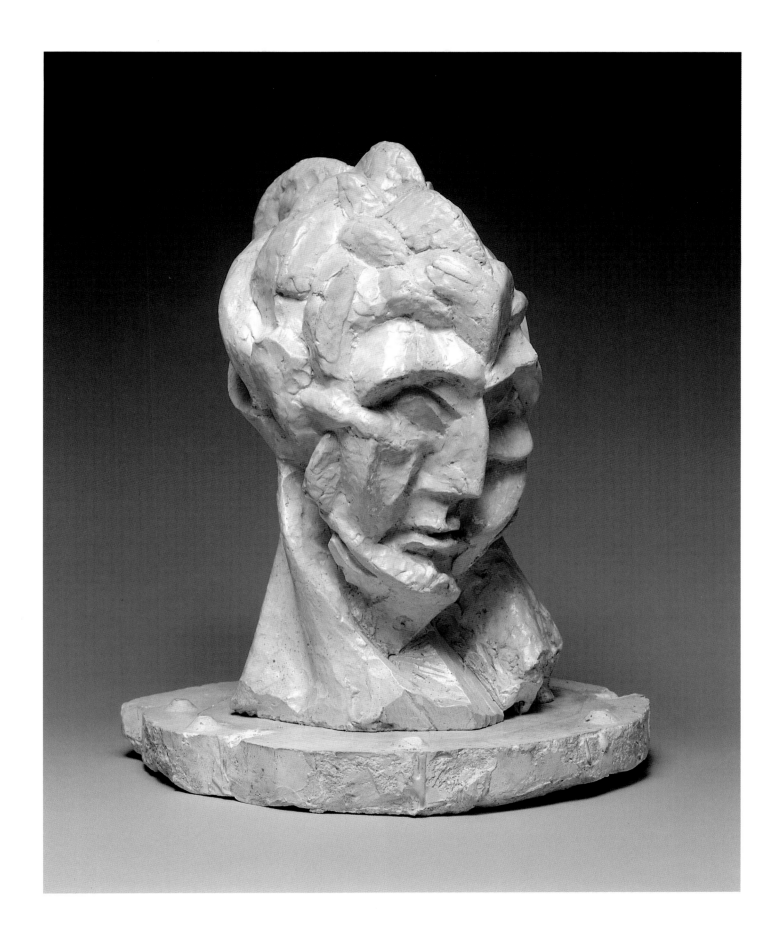

PABLO PICASSO

Pregnant Woman (second state) (La Femme enceinte [2ème état]), 1950/59

Bronze

42 3/4 x 11 3/8 x 13 1/4 inches (108.6 x 28.9 x 33.7 cm)

Marked 2/2

PABLO PICASSO

Flowers in a Vase (Fleurs dans un vase), 1951–53

Plaster, terra-cotta, and iron

30 1/8 x 20 1/4 x 17 1/4 inches (76.5 x 51.4 x 43.8 cm)

RAYMOND DUCHAMP-VILLON

Torso of a Young Man (Le Torse de jeune homme), also called **The Athlete**, 1910

Terra-cotta

22 3/8 x 12 3/4 x 16 1/2 inches (56.8 x 32.4 x 41.9 cm)

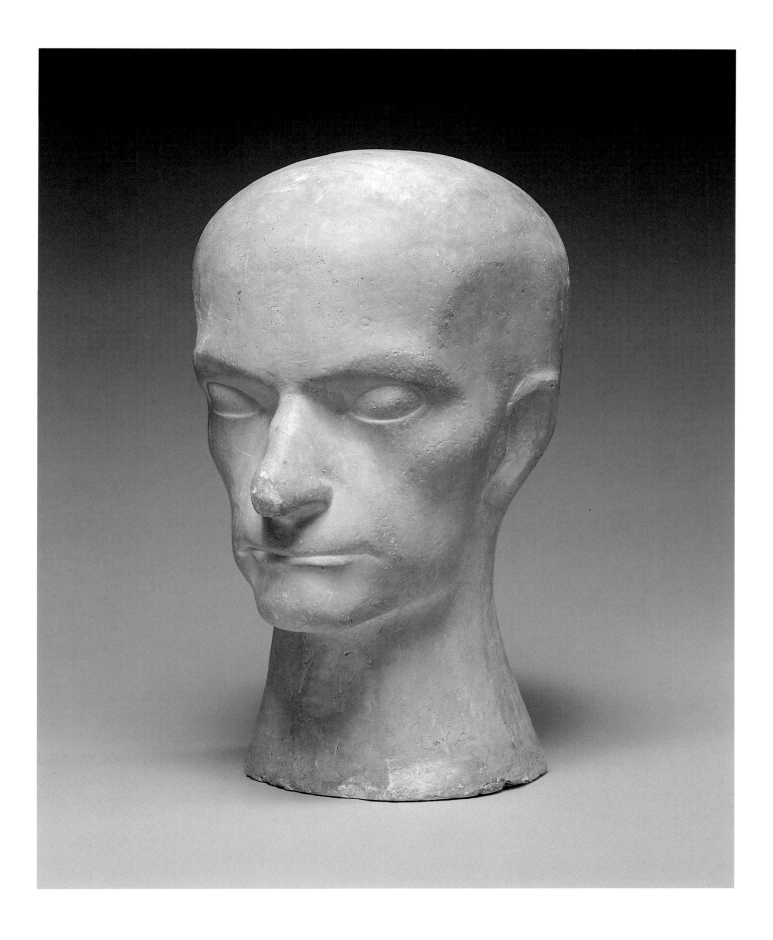

RAYMOND DUCHAMP-VILLON

Maggy, 1912

Bronze

28 x 13 1/4 x 15 inches (71.1 x 33.7 x 38.1 cm)

Marked 4/8, cast 1957

RAYMOND DUCHAMP-VILLON

Cat (Le Chat), 1913

Plaster

25 ¹/₂ x 21 ¹/₂ x 3 ¹/₄ inches (64.8 x 54.6 x 8.3 cm)

RAYMOND DUCHAMP-VILLON

Horse and Rider II (Cheval et cavalier II), 1914

Bronze

10 3/4 x 7 1/2 x 4 inches (27.3 x 19 x 10.2 cm)

RAYMOND DUCHAMP-VILLON

Large Horse (Le Cheval majeur), 1914

(second enlargement, by Marcel Duchamp, fabricated 1966)

Bronze

59 ½ x 57 x 34 inches (151.1 x 144.8 x 86.4 cm)

Marked 7/9

RAYMOND DUCHAMP-VILLON

Portrait of Professor Gosset (Portrait du Professeur Gosset), 1918

Bronze

3 3/8 x 3 1/4 x 3 3/8 inches (8.6 x 8.3 x 8.6 cm)

Marked 5/9, cast 1960s

GASTON LACHAISE

Elevation, also called **Standing Woman**, 1912–27

Bronze

70 3/4 x 30 x 19 9/16 inches (179.7 x 76.2 x 49.7 cm)

Marked 2/4, cast 1964

HENRI GAUDIER-BRZESKA

Hieratic Head of Ezra Pound, 1914

Marble

35 5/8 x 18 x 19 1/4 inches (90.5 x 45.7 x 48.9 cm)

ALEXANDER ARCHIPENKO

Woman Combing Her Hair (Femme debout), 1914 or 1915

Bronze

14 1/8 x 3 5/8 x 3 3/16 inches (35.9 x 9.2 x 8.1 cm)

ALEXANDER ARCHIPENKO

Torso in Space, also called **Floating Torso,** 1935

Bronze

6 3/4 x 22 1/2 x 5 1/2 inches (17.1 x 57.2 x 14 cm)

Marked 5

IVAN PUNI

Construction Relief, ca. 1915–16

Painted wood and tin, mounted on wood
22 7/8 x 18 3/8 x 3 1/2 inches (58.1 x 46.7 x 8.9 cm)

JACQUES LIPCHITZ

Seated Woman (Cubist Figure), 1916

Stone

42 1/2 x 11 1/4 x 12 1/4 inches (108 x 28.6 x 31.1 cm)

ALBERTO GIACOMETTI

Spoon Woman (Femme cuillère), 1926

Bronze

56 3/4 x 20 x 9 inches (144 x 51 x 23 cm)

Marked 2/6, cast 1954

ALBERTO GIACOMETTI

Woman (Femme), ca. 1927–28

Bronze

14 1/4 x 6 7/8 x 3 1/2 inches (36.2 x 17.5 x 8.9 cm)

Marked 2/6

ALBERTO GIACOMETTI

No More Play (On ne joue plus), 1931–32

Marble, wood, and bronze

1 5/8 x 22 7/8 x 17 3/4 inches (4.1 x 58.1 x 45.1 cm)

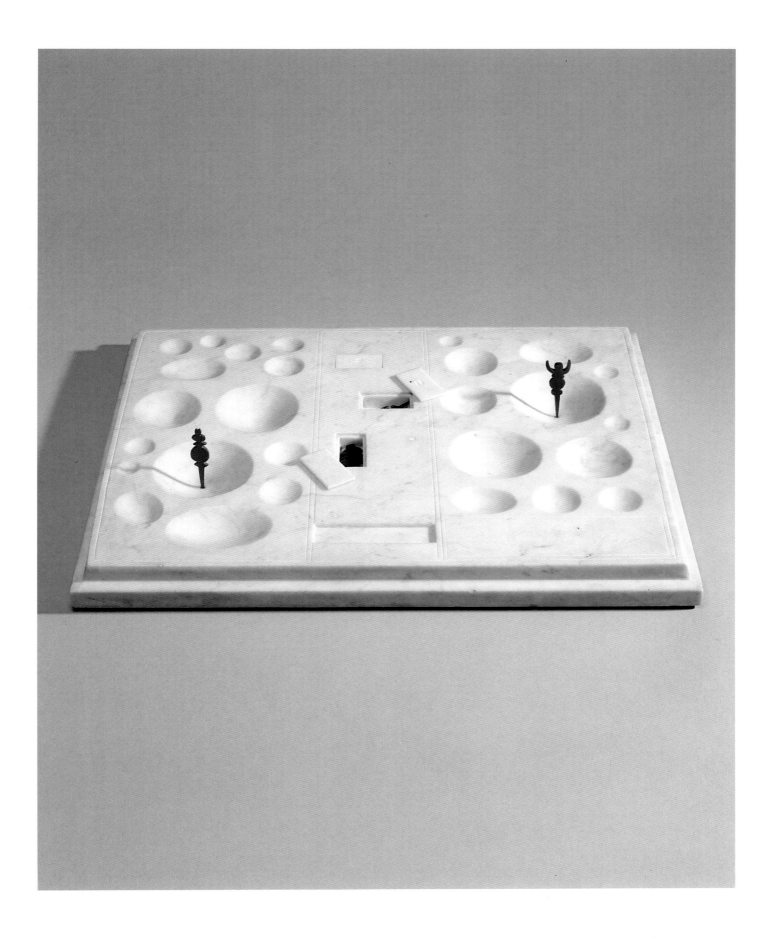

ALBERTO GIACOMETTI

Cubist Head (Tête dite cubiste), 1934

Marble

7 3/8 x 7 3/4 x 8 1/8 inches (18.7 x 19.7 x 20.6 cm)

ALBERTO GIACOMETTI

Two Figurines (Deux figurines sur socles), ca. 1945

Gold leaf over metal

Two pieces, 1 7/16 x 7/16 x 7/16 inches (3.7 x 1.1 x 1.1 cm) each

ALBERTO GIACOMETTI

The Chariot (Le Chariot), 1950

Painted bronze

56 1/4 x 24 1/4 x 27 inches (142.9 x 61.6 x 68.6 cm)

The Patsy and Raymond Nasher Collection at The Nelson-Atkins Museum of Art,

Kansas City, Missouri, Lent by the Hall Family Foundation

Marked 5/6

ALBERTO GIACOMETTI

Bust of Diego (Buste de Diego), 1954 (two views)

Painted bronze

15 1/2 x 13 1/4 x 8 1/4 inches (39.4 x 33.7 x 21 cm)

Marked 0/6

(pages 156–57)

ALBERTO GIACOMETTI

Diego in a Cloak (Diego au manteau), 1954

Painted bronze

15 1/8 x 13 1/2 x 8 3/4 inches (38.4 x 34.3 x 22.2 cm)

Marked 6/6

ALBERTO GIACOMETTI

Diego in a Sweater (Diego au chandail), 1953

Painted bronze

19 x 10 ¾ x 8 ¼ inches (48.3 x 27.3 x 21 cm)

Marked 6/6

ALBERTO GIACOMETTI

Venice Woman III (Femme de Venise III), 1956

Bronze

47 1/2 x 13 1/2 x 6 7/8 inches (120.7 x 34.3 x 17.5 cm)

Marked 0/6

ALBERTO GIACOMETTI

Head of Diego on Base (Tête de Diego sur socle), 1958

Bronze
12 x 3 3/8 x 4 1/4 inches (30.5 x 8.6 x 10.8 cm)
Marked 1/6

JOHN STORRS

Study in Architectural Forms (Forms in Space), 1927

Steel

31 3/16 x 7 5/8 x 4 5/8 inches (79.2 x 19.4 x 11.7 cm)

JULIO GONZÁLEZ

Mask: Reclining Head (Masque: Tête couchée), ca. 1930

Iron

6 1/4 x 7 1/4 x 4 1/2 inches (16 x 18.5 x 11.5 cm)

JULIO GONZÁLEZ

Woman with a Mirror (Femme au miroir), ca. 1936–37

Bronze

6 feet 8 15/16 inches x 2 feet 2 3/8 inches x 1 foot 2 3/16 inches (2.04 x .67 x .36 m)

Marked 1/2, cast ca. 1980

HENRI LAURENS

Grande Maternité, 1932

Bronze
21 1/2 x 55 x 22 1/2 inches (54.6 x 139.7 x 57.2 cm)
Marked 0/6, cast 1965

DAVID SMITH

Head, 1938

Welded iron, painted red, on wood base

17 7/16 x 8 x 7 inches (44.3 x 20.3 x 17.8 cm)

DAVID SMITH

House in a Landscape (Rural Landscape with Manless House), 1945

Steel

18 1/2 x 24 3/4 x 6 inches (47 x 62.9 x 15.2 cm)

DAVID SMITH

Perfidious Albion (The British Empire), 1945

Bronze, cast iron, green patina made with acid

14 3/8 x 4 1/2 x 2 5/8 inches (36.5 x 11.4 x 6.7 cm)

Marked 3/3

DAVID SMITH

The Forest, 1950

Steel, painted green and pink, on wood base

38 ¹/₄ x 39 x 4 inches (97.2 x 99.1 x 10.2 cm)

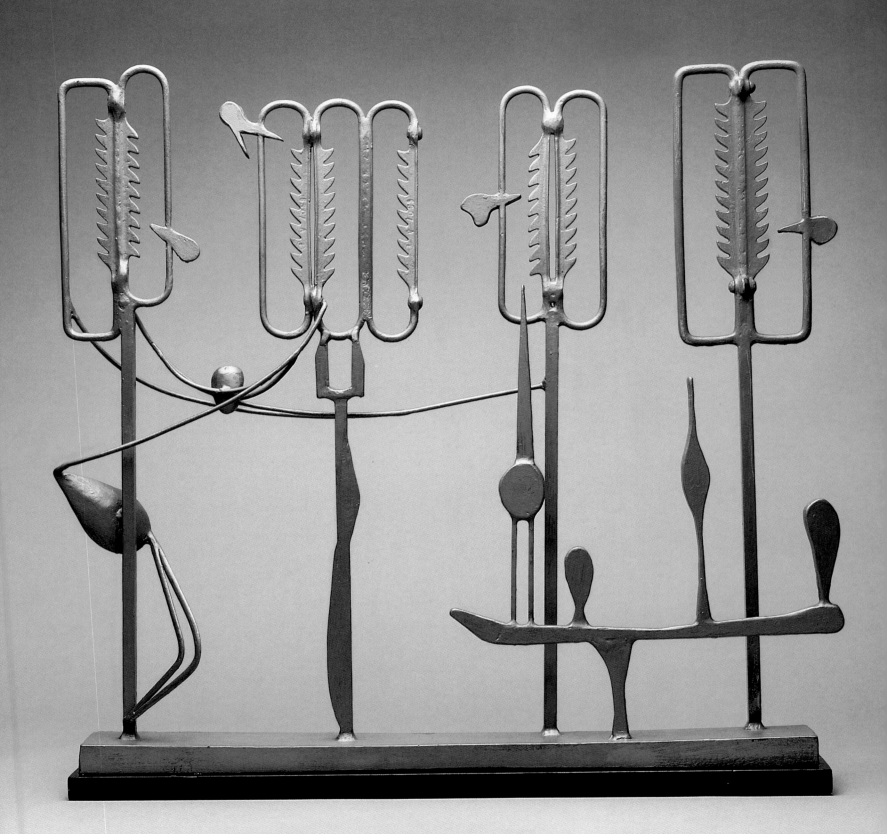

DAVID SMITH

9/15/53, 1953

Steel, on iron base

21 1/2 x 37 3/4 x 13 inches (54.6 x 95.9 x 33 cm)

DAVID SMITH

Tower Eight, 1957

Silver

46 1/2 x 13 x 10 5/8 inches (118.1 x 33 x 27 cm)

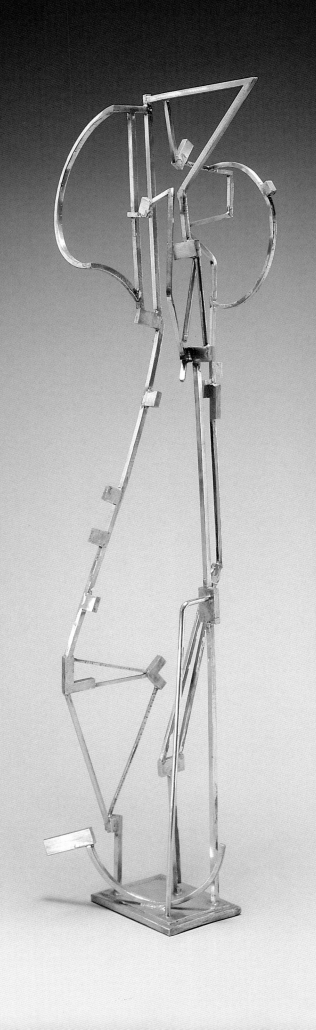

DAVID SMITH

Untitled (Voltri), 1962

Steel

41 1/4 x 14 5/8 x 7 1/8 inches (104.8 x 37.1 x 18.1 cm)

DAVID SMITH

Voltri VI, 1962

Steel

8 feet 2 7/8 inches x 8 feet 6 1/4 inches x 2 feet (2.51 x 2.6 x .61 m)

GEORGES BRAQUE

Hymen, 1939

Bronze

29 5/8 x 20 1/8 x 13 inches (75.2 x 51.1 x 33 cm)

Marked 2/6, cast 1957

ALEXANDER CALDER

The Spider, 1940

Sheet metal and steel rod, painted

7 feet 11 inches x 8 feet 3 inches x 6 feet 1 inch (2.41 x 2.52 x 1.85 m)

ALEXANDER CALDER

Mobile, 1958

Sheet metal and steel wire, painted
6 x 9 x 4 feet (1.83 x 2.74 x 1.22 m)

ALEXANDER CALDER

Three Bollards (Trois Bollards), 1970

Painted steel
11 feet 5 inches x 9 feet 6 inches x 11 feet 5 inches (3.48 x 2.9 x 3.48 m)
(pages 196–97)

NAUM GABO

Linear Construction in Space No. 1 (Variation), 1942–43

(enlargement, ca. 1957–58)

Plexiglas with nylon monofilament

24 3/4 x 24 3/4 x 9 1/2 inches (62.9 x 62.9 x 24.1 cm)

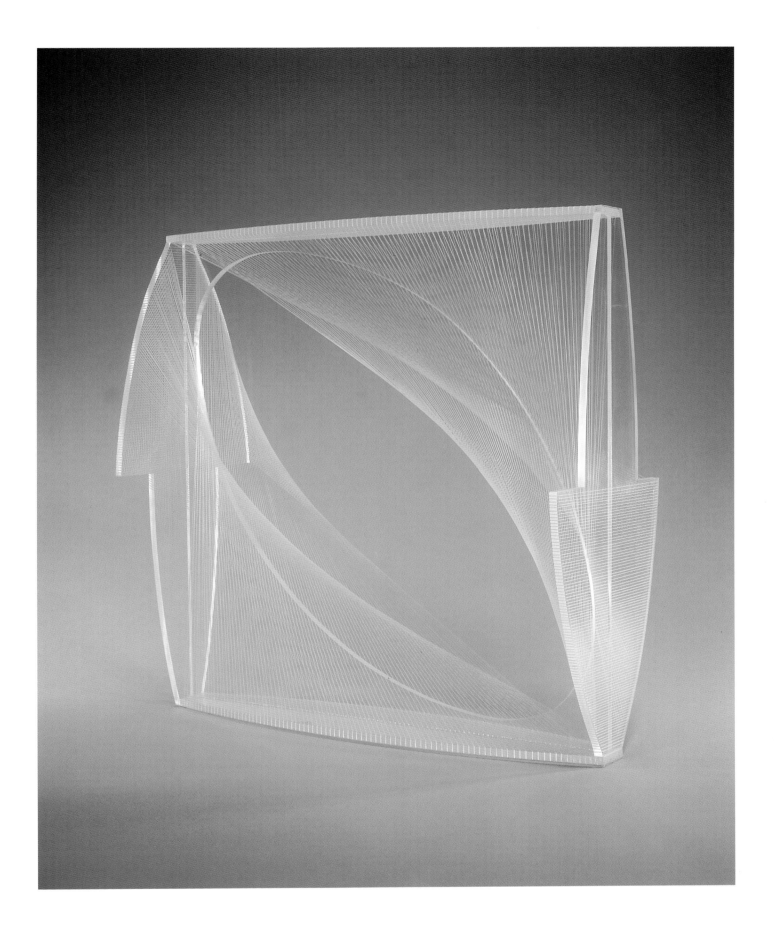

MAX ERNST

The Table Is Set (La Table est mise), 1944

Bronze

12 x 24 ½ x 21 ¾ inches (30.5 x 62.2 x 55.2 cm)

Cast 1955

MAX ERNST

The King Playing with the Queen, 1944

Bronze

37 7/8 x 33 x 21 1/8 inches (96.2 x 83.8 x 53.7 cm)

Marked 3/9, cast 1954

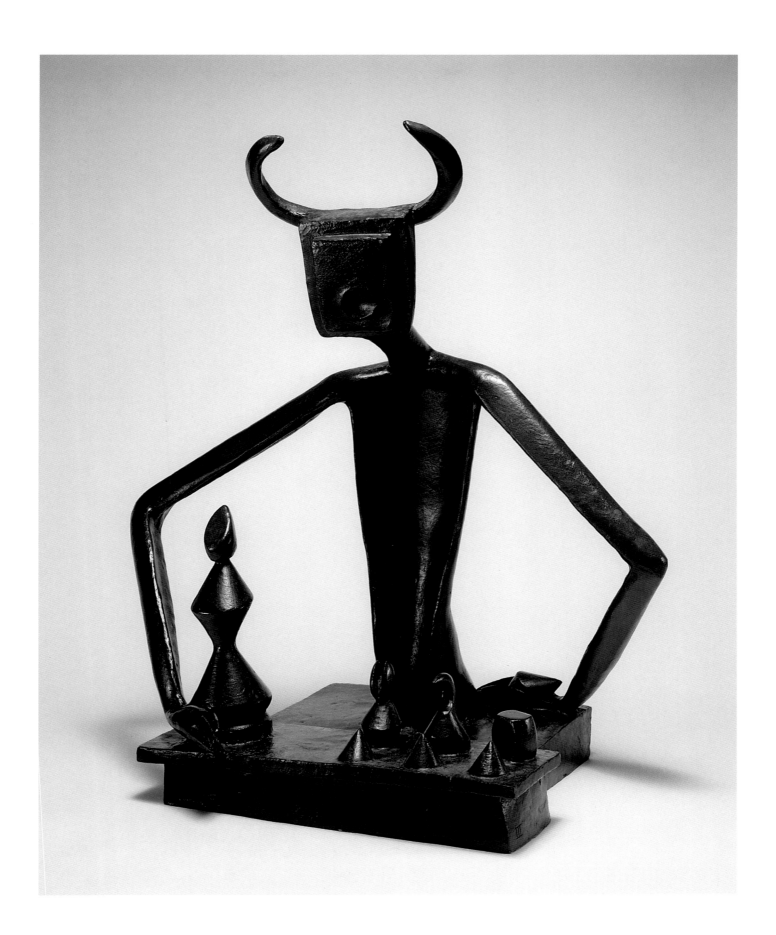

MAX ERNST

Capricorn, 1948

Bronze

7 feet 5 inches x 6 feet 10 inches x 4 feet 7 1/4 inches (2.26 x 2.08 x 1.4 m)

The Patsy and Raymond Nasher Collection at The Nelson-Atkins Museum of Art,

Kansas City, Missouri, Lent by the Hall Family Foundation

Marked 0/5, cast 1963–64

MAX ERNST

The Spirit of the Bastille (Le Génie de la Bastille), 1960

Bronze
10 feet 3 ¼ inches x 1 foot x 1 foot 1 inch (3.13 x .31 x .33 m)
Marked E.A. (artist's proof) 2/3, cast 1961

MAX ERNST

Sister Souls (Âmes–soeurs), 1961

Bronze

36 5/8 x 12 x 12 1/2 inches (93 x 30.5 x 31.8 cm)

Marked E.A. (artist's proof) 2/3

JOAN MIRÓ

Moonbird (Oiseau lunaire), 1944–46 (enlargement, 1966)

Bronze

7 feet 6 inches x 6 feet 8 1/2 inches x 4 feet 9 3/4 inches (2.29 x 2.05 x 1.47 m)

Marked 4/5, cast 1967

JOAN MIRÓ

Caress of a Bird (La Caresse d'un oiseau), 1967

Painted bronze

10 feet 3 inches x 3 feet 7 1/2 inches x 1 foot 7 inches (3.12 x 1.11 x .48 m)

Marked 4/4

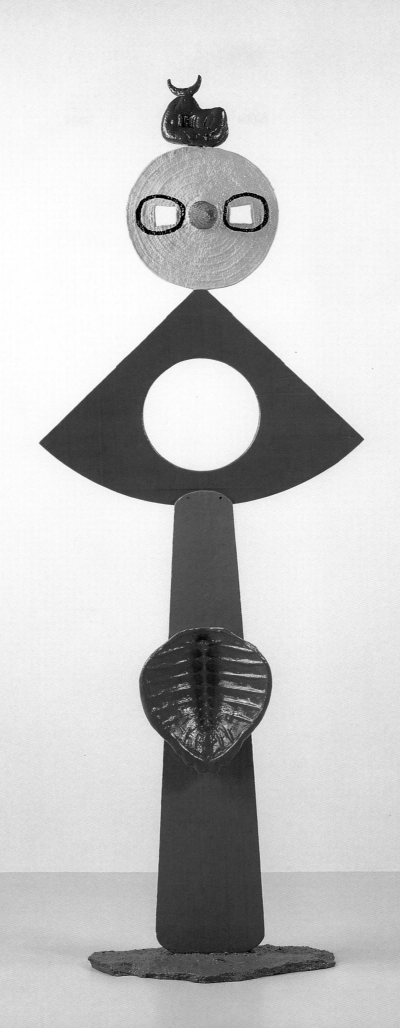

JOAN MIRÓ

Seated Woman and Child (Femme assise et enfant), 1967

Painted bronze

48 1/4 x 16 3/4 x 16 1/2 inches (122.6 x 42.5 x 41.9 cm)

Marked N 4

ISAMU NOGUCHI

Gregory (Effigy), 1945

Bronze
69 1/4 x 16 1/8 x 16 3/8 inches (175.9 x 41 x 41.6 cm)
Marked 4/8, cast 1969

ANTOINE PEVSNER

Dynamic Projection at Thirty Degrees

(Projection dynamique au 30ᵉ degré), 1950–51

Bronze

3 feet 1 1/8 inches x 6 feet 2 1/4 inches x 3 feet (.94 x 1.89 x .91 m)

Marked 3/3, cast after 1960

JEAN DUBUFFET

Le Fuligineux, 1954

Lava rock and slag

14 1/2 x 8 1/4 x 6 1/4 inches (36.8 x 21 x 15.9 cm)

JEAN DUBUFFET

The Gossiper II (Le Deviseur II), 1969–70 (enlargement, 1984)

Painted polyester resin

10 feet x 6 feet 9 3/4 inches x 7 feet 1 1/4 inches (3.05 x 2.08 x 2.17 m)

JEAN DUBUFFET

Tour dentellière, 1973–81

Cast epoxy painted with polyurethane

7 feet 10 ½ inches x 3 feet 9 inches x 3 feet 3 inches (2.4 x 1.19 x .99 m)

JOHN CHAMBERLAIN

Zaar, 1959

Welded steel, painted

51 1/4 x 68 3/8 x 19 5/8 inches (130.2 x 173.7 x 49.8 cm)

JOHN CHAMBERLAIN

Williamson Turn, 1974

Painted and chromium-plated steel
46 x 37 x 48 inches (116.8 x 94 x 121.9 cm)

CLAES OLDENBURG

Mannikin Torso: Two-Piece Bathing Suit, 1960

Muslin soaked in plaster over wire frame, painted

32 ¹/₂ x 14 ³/₄ x 4 ¹/₂ inches (82.6 x 37.5 x 11.4 cm)

CLAES OLDENBURG

Typewriter Eraser, 1976

Stainless steel, ferrocement, and aluminum, on steel base
7 feet 5 inches x 7 feet 6 inches x 5 feet 3 inches (2.26 x 2.29 x 1.6 m)
Marked 2/3

JEAN ARP

Torso with Buds (Nu aux bourgeons), 1961

Bronze
6 feet 1 7/8 inches x 1 foot 3 1/2 inches x 1 foot 3 inches (1.88 x .39 x .38 m)
Marked 1/3

ANTHONY CARO

Sculpture Three, 1961

Painted steel
9 feet 10 inches x 14 feet 6 1/2 inches x 4 feet 3 inches (3 x 4.43 x 1.3 m)
(pages 236–37)

ANTHONY CARO

Carriage, 1966

Painted steel
6 feet 5 inches x 6 feet 8 inches x 13 feet (1.96 x 2.03 x 3.96 m)
(pages 238–39)

ANTHONY CARO

Fanshoal, 1971–72

Painted steel

63 x 70 x 31 inches (160 x 177.8 x 78.7 cm)

TONY SMITH

The Snake Is Out, 1962 (fabricated 1981)

Painted steel

15 feet x 23 feet 2 inches x 18 feet 10 inches (4.57 x 7.06 x 5.74 m)

Marked 1/3

(pages 242–43)

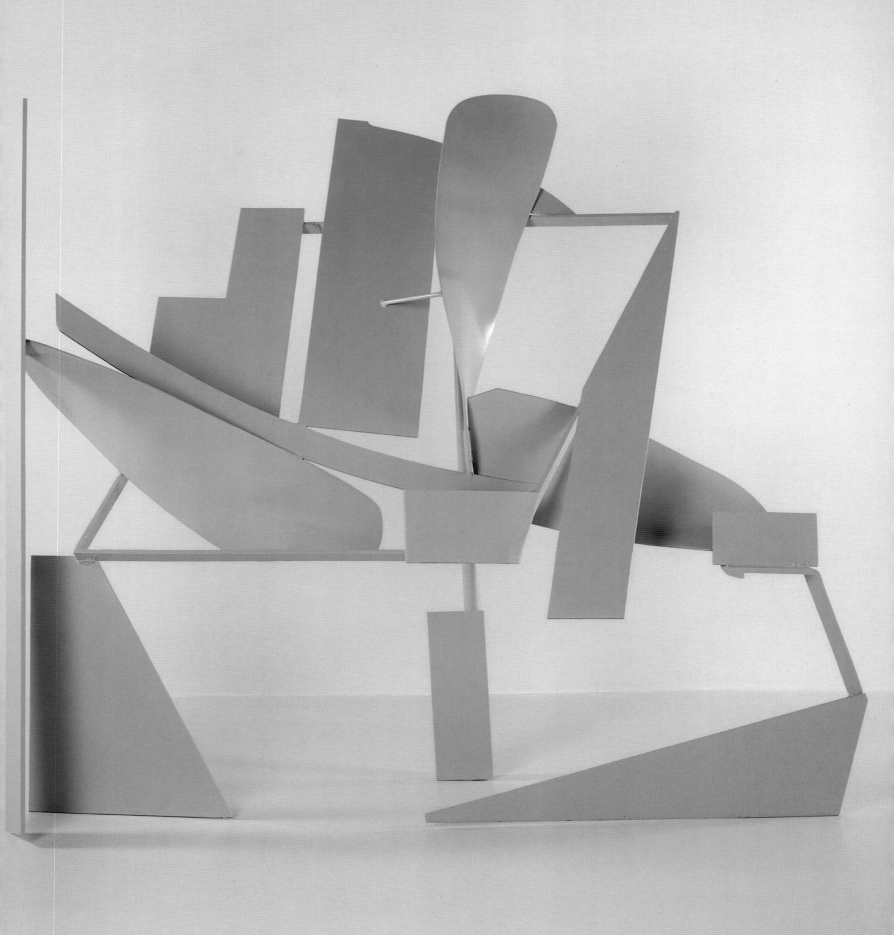

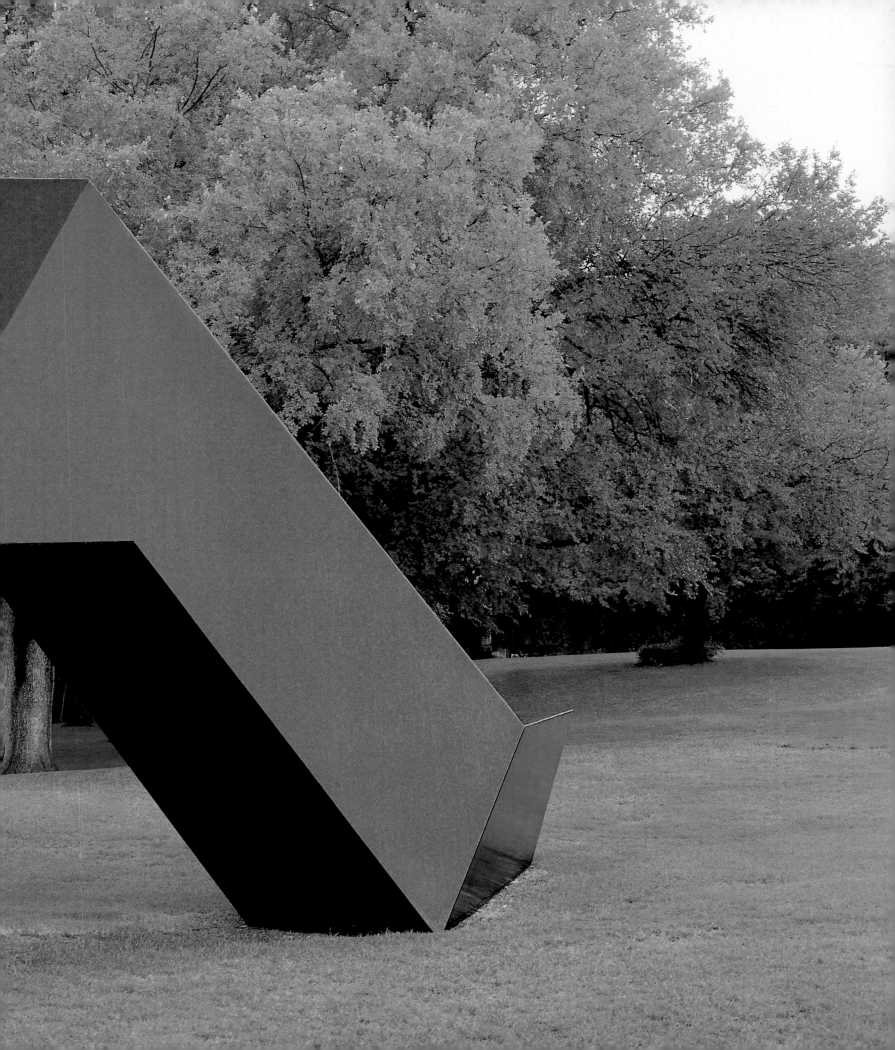

TONY SMITH

For Dolores, also called **Flores para los muertos,** ca. 1973–75

Carrara marble

44 ¹/₄ x 44 ³/₄ x 45 ¹/₄ inches (112.4 x 113.7 x 114.9 cm)

TONY SMITH

Ten Elements, 1975–79 (fabricated 1980)

Painted aluminum

Ten pieces; tallest piece: 50 inches (127 cm) high;
shortest piece: 42 inches (106.7 cm) high

(pages 246–47)

BARBARA HEPWORTH

Squares with Two Circles (Monolith), 1963

Bronze

10 feet 4 inches x 5 feet 5 inches x 2 feet 6 inches (3.15 x 1.65 x .76 m)

Marked 3/3, cast 1964

BARNETT NEWMAN

Here III, 1965–66

Stainless and Cor–Ten steel
10 feet 11 inches x 1 foot 11 1/2 inches x 1 foot 6 5/8 inches (3.18 x .6 x .47 m)
Marked B/3

HENRY MOORE

Three Piece No. 3: Vertebrae, 1968

Polished bronze
3 feet 5 1/8 inches x 7 feet 9 inches x 4 feet (1.05 x 2.36 x 1.22 m)
Marked 4/8

(pages 252–53)

HENRY MOORE

Working Model for Oval with Points, 1968–69

Bronze with brown patina

44 x 40 x 36 inches (111.8 x 101.6 x 91.4 cm)

Marked 5/12

HENRY MOORE

Reclining Figure: Angles, 1979

Bronze

4 feet 1/4 inch x 7 feet 6 1/4 inches x 5 feet 1 3/4 inches (1.23 x 2.29 x 1.57 m)

Marked 4/9, cast 1980

(pages 256–57)

CARL ANDRE

Aluminum and Magnesium Plain, 1969

Aluminum and magnesium
Thirty-six plates, 3/8 inch x 6 feet x 6 feet (.01 x 1.83 x 1.83 m) overall
The Patsy and Raymond Nasher Collection at The Nelson-Atkins Museum of Art,
Kansas City, Missouri, Lent by the Hall Family Foundation

RICHARD SERRA

Inverted House of Cards, 1969–70

Cor–Ten steel

Four pieces, 4 feet 7 1/4 inches x 4 feet 7 1/4 inches x 1 inch (1.4 x 1.4 x .03 m) each;
4 feet 7 1/4 inches x 8 feet 5 3/4 inches x 8 feet 5 1/2 inches (1.4 x 2.58 x 2.58 m) overall

RICHARD SERRA

My Curves Are Not Mad, 1987

Cor–Ten steel

Two plates, 14 feet x 44 ft 11 3/8 inches x 2 inches (4.27 x 13.7 x .05 m) each;
distance between plates: 11 feet 3 inches (3.43 m) at widest point

(pages 262–63)

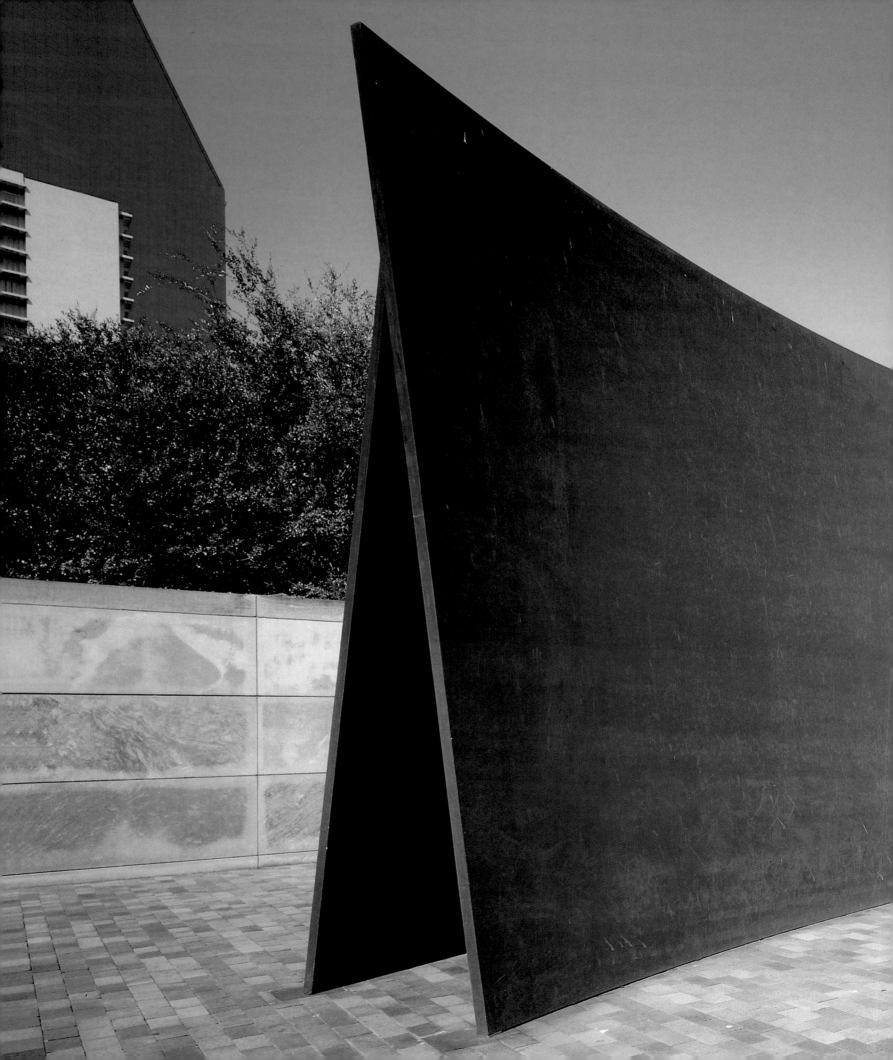

WILLEM DE KOONING

Seated Woman, 1969

Bronze

9 feet 5 inches x 12 feet 3 inches x 7 feet 10 inches (2.87 x 3.73 x 2.39 m)

Marked 2/7, cast 1980

WILLEM DE KOONING

Hostess (Bar Girl), 1973

Bronze
48 3/4 x 38 x 25 3/4 inches (123.8 x 96.5 x 65.4 cm)
Marked 7/7

MARK DI SUVERO

In the Bushes, 1970–75

Painted steel

11 feet 10 inches x 10 feet 6 inches x 6 feet 9 inches (3.61 x 3.2 x 2.06 m)

MARK DI SUVERO

For W. B. Yeats, 1985–87

Steel

8 feet 4 3/4 inches x 11 feet 11 7/16 inches x 7 feet 4 5/16 inches (2.56 x 3.64 x 2.24 m)

CHRISTOPHER WILMARTH

My Divider, 1972–73

Glass and steel

5 feet x 6 feet 6 inches x 7 feet 10 inches (1.52 x 1.98 x 2.39 m)

JOEL SHAPIRO

Untitled, 1975

Cast iron

6 3/8 x 10 5/8 x 9 1/4 inches (16.2 x 27 x 23.5 cm)

JOEL SHAPIRO

Untitled, 1983

Bronze
7 feet 1 3/4 inches x 5 feet x 3 feet (2.18 x 1.52 x .91 m)
Marked 1/3

JOEL SHAPIRO

Untitled, 1985–87

Bronze

9 feet 9 3/4 inches x 9 feet 3 1/4 inches x 8 feet 2 inches (2.99 x 2.83 x 2.49 m)

Marked 3/3

JOEL SHAPIRO

Untitled, 1986

Painted wood

65 1/8 x 59 1/2 x 48 1/2 inches (165.4 x 151.1 x 123.2 cm)

DONALD JUDD

Untitled, 1976

Aluminum and anodized aluminum

8 1/4 inches x 13 feet 5 inches x 8 inches (.21 x 4.09 x .2 m)

(pages 282–83)

WILLIAM TUCKER

Building a Wall in the Air, 1978

Mild steel

9 feet 11 inches x 7 feet 3 inches x 1 foot 3 inches (3.02 x 2.21 x .38 m)

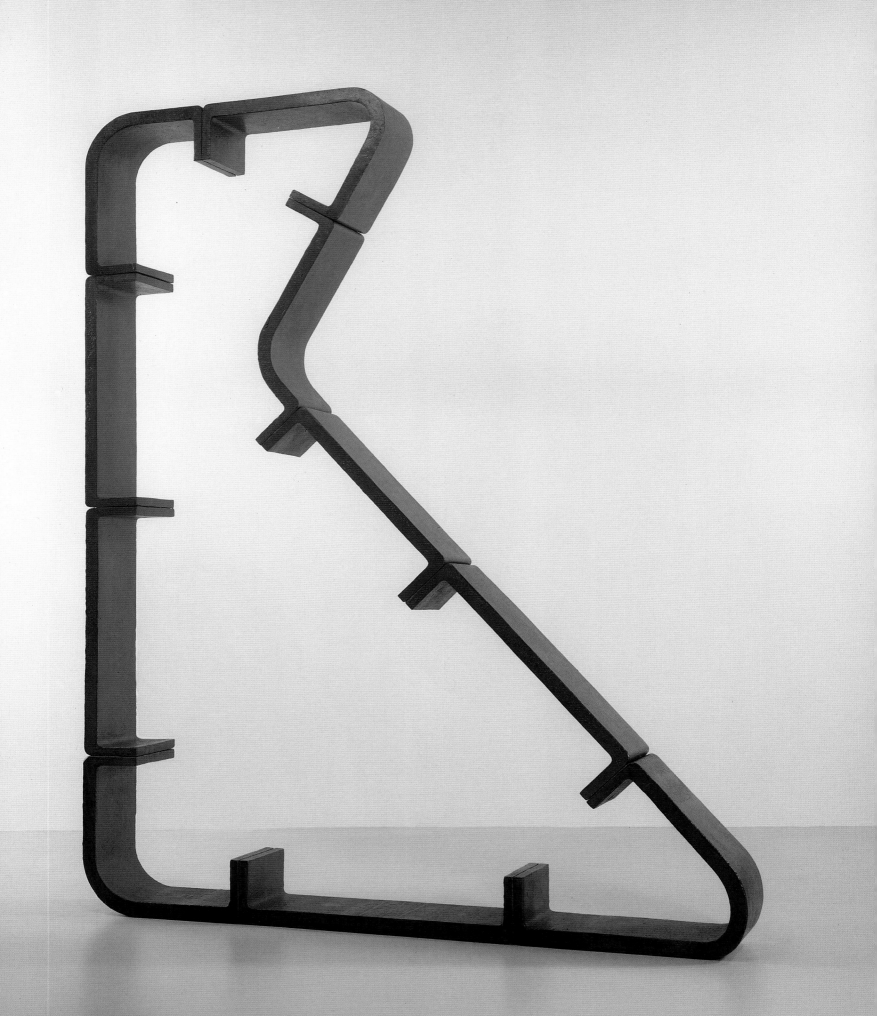

ROY LICHTENSTEIN

Double Glass, 1979

Painted and patinated bronze
56 x 42 x 17 inches (142.2 x 106.6 x 43.1 cm)
Marked 2/3

ALAIN KIRILI

Commandment V, 1980

Forged iron
Seventeen pieces; tallest piece: 12 ¹/₂ x 6 x 7 inches (31.8 x 15.2 x 17.8 cm)
(pages 288–89)

ULRICH RÜCKRIEM

Untitled (#7), 1980

Texas red granite
Four pieces, 2 feet 5 inches x 8 feet 10 ¹/₄ inches x 3 feet 4 inches
(.74 x 2.7 x 1.02 m) overall
(pages 290–91)

BARRY FLANAGAN

Large Leaping Hare, 1982

Gold leaf over bronze, on painted tubular-steel base

9 feet 2 inches x 9 feet 3 inches x 3 feet 8 inches (2.79 x 2.82 x 1.12 m)

ANTONY GORMLEY

Three Places, 1983

Lead, fiberglass, and plaster

Lying figure: 1 foot x 6 feet 8 inches x 1 foot 7 inches (.31 x 2.03 x .48 m);

seated figure: 3 feet 3 inches x 4 feet 3 inches x 1 foot 10 inches (.99 x 1.3 x .56 m);

standing figure: 6 feet 2 inches x 1 foot 7 inches x 1 foot 1 inch (1.88 x .48 x .33 m)

GEORGE SEGAL

Rush Hour, 1983 (two views)

Bronze

6 feet 1 inch x 6 feet 2 inches x 5 feet 7 inches (1.85 x 1.88 x 1.7 m)

Cast 1985–86

(pages 296–97)

SCOTT BURTON

Schist Furniture Group (Settee with Two Chairs), 1983–84

Schist

Settee: 39 x 71 x 47 ¹/₂ inches (99.1 x 180.3 x 120.7 cm);

two chairs: 43 x 28 x 32 inches (109.2 x 71.1 x 81.3 cm) and 39 x 27 ¹/₂ x 35 inches (99.1 x 69.8 x 88.9 cm)

(pages 298–99)

RICHARD DEACON

Like a Bird, 1984

Laminated wood

10 feet 1 inch x 17 feet 4 inches x 17 feet 1 inch (3.07 x 5.28 x 5.21 m)

(pages 300–01)

ANISH KAPOOR

In Search of the Mountain I, 1984

Wood, gesso, and pigment

3 feet 4 7/8 inches x 3 feet 4 7/8 inches x 8 feet 4 inches (1.14 x 1.14 x 2.54 m)

MARTIN PURYEAR

Night and Day, 1984

Painted wood and wire

6 feet 11 1/2 inches x 9 feet 10 1/2 inches x 5 inches (2.12 x 3.01 x .13 m)

(pages 304–05)

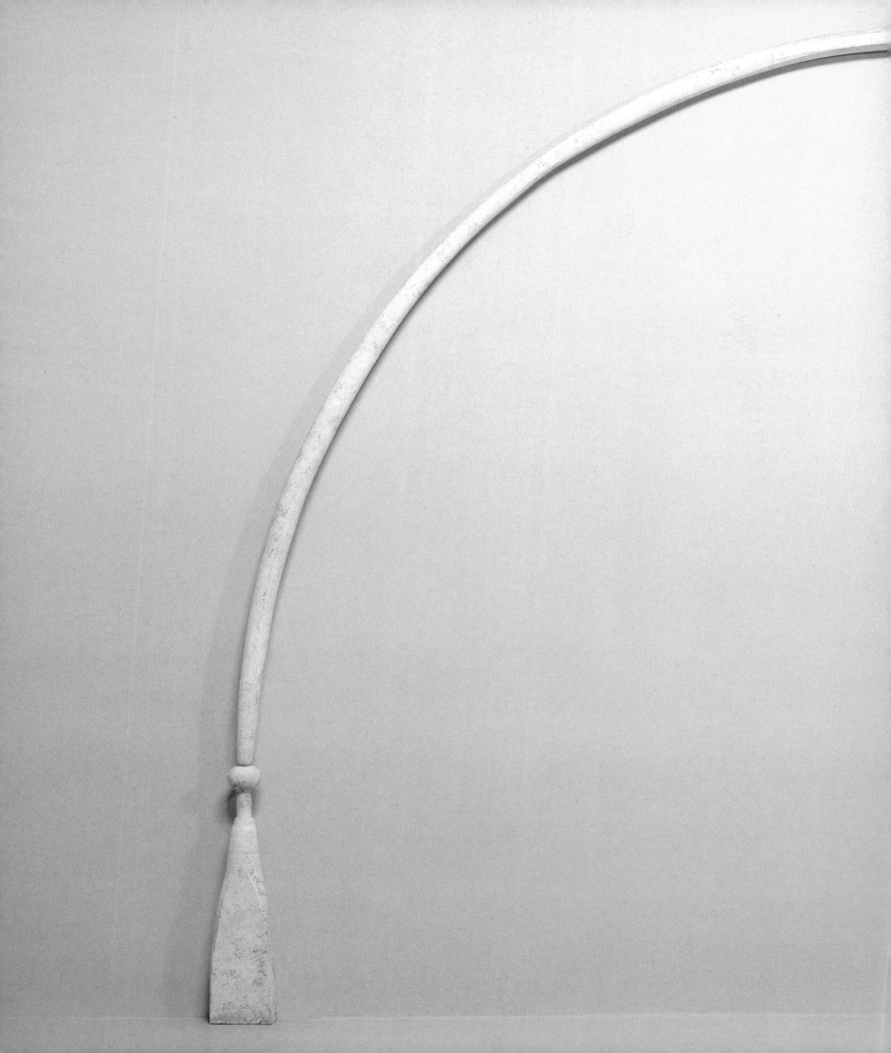

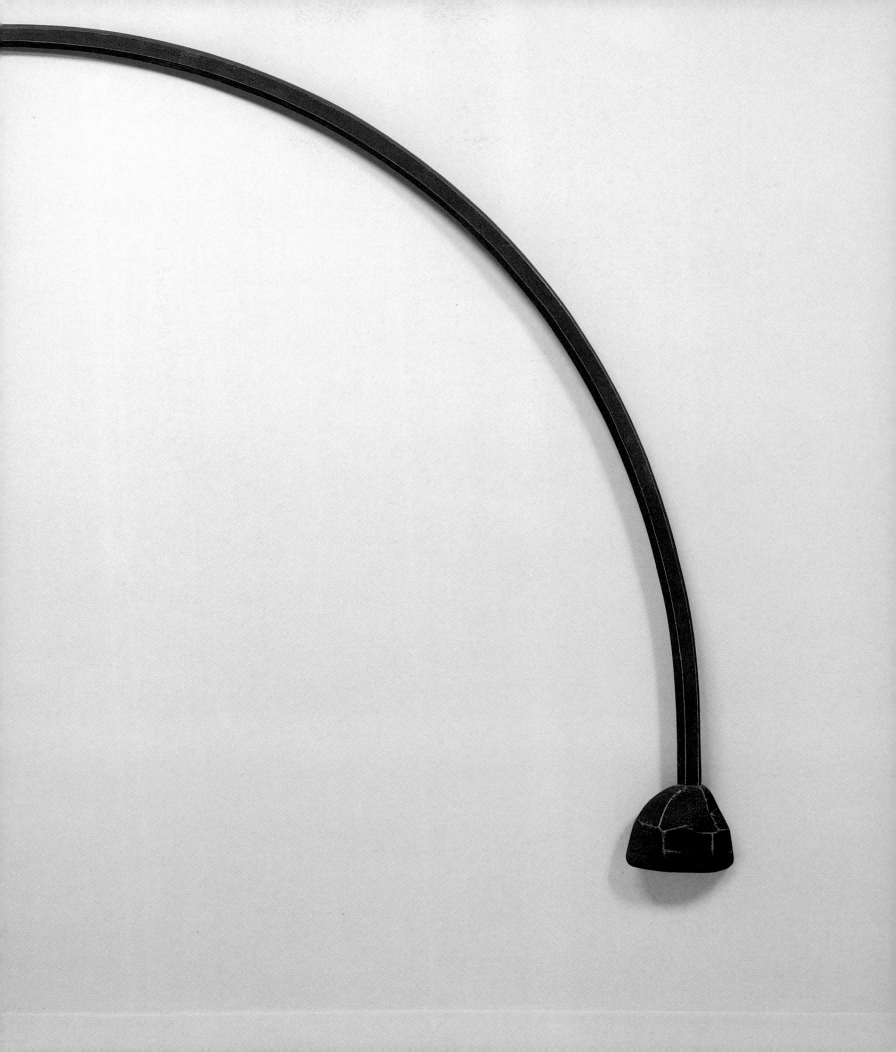

JONATHAN BOROFSKY

Hammering Man, 1984–85

Painted steel plate and Cor–Ten steel

20 feet x 9 feet x 1 foot 6 ¹/₂ inches (6.1 x 2.74 x .47 m)

JEFF KOONS

Louis XIV, 1986

Stainless steel
46 x 27 x 15 inches (116.8 x 68.6 x 38.1 cm)
Marked 3/3

TONY CRAGG

Glass Instruments, 1987

Eroded glass, wood, and metal

6 feet 10 5/8 inches x 5 feet 6 7/8 inches x 4 feet 7 1/8 inches (2.1 x 1.7 x 1.4 m)

ELLSWORTH KELLY

Untitled, 1986

Bronze

9 feet 11 7/8 inches x 1 foot 5 5/16 inches x 1 1/4 inches (3.05 x .44 x .03 m)

MAGDALENA ABAKANOWICZ

Bronze Crowd, 1990–91

Bronze

Thirty-six pieces, approximately 71 1/8 x 23 x 15 1/2 inches (180.7 x 58.4 x 39.4 cm) each

(pages 314–15)

RICHARD LONG

Midsummer Circles, 1993

Delabole slate

17 feet 4 inches (5.28 m) in diameter

(pages 316–17)

ALBERTO GIACOMETTI

Three Personages (Trois personnages),

also called **Three Figures in the Street** (**Trois figures dans la rue**), 1949

Oil on canvas

22 1/16 x 18 5/16 inches (56 x 46.5 cm)

PABLO PICASSO

The Studio (L'Atelier), 1961–62

Oil on canvas

29 x 36 inches (73.7 x 91.4 cm)

PABLO PICASSO

The Kiss (Le Baiser), 1969

Oil on canvas

38 1/8 x 51 3/16 inches (96.8 x 130 cm)

PABLO PICASSO

Vase of Flowers on a Table (Bouquet)

(Vase de fleurs sur une table [bouquet]), 1969

Oil on canvas

45 1/2 x 35 inches (115.6 x 88.9 cm)

PABLO PICASSO

Nude Man and Woman (Homme et femme nus), 1971

Oil on canvas

6 feet 4 5/8 inches x 4 feet 3 1/8 inches (1.95 x 1.3 m)

JEAN DUBUFFET

Conjugaison, 1975

Acrylic on paper, mounted on cloth

4 feet 4 3/8 inches x 9 feet 11 3/4 inches (1.33 x 3.04 m)

(pages 328–29)

INDEX OF REPRODUCTIONS